Creation and Fall

TWO BIBLICAL STUDIES

Temptation

DIETRICH BONHOEFFER

A TOUCHSTONE BOOK
PUBLISHED BY SIMON & SCHUSTER

TOUCHSTONE
Rockefeller Center
1230 Avenue of the Americas
New York, NY 10020

First Touchstone Edition 1997
Published by arrangement with SCM Press Ltd

TOUCHSTONE and colophon are registered trademarks
of Simon & Schuster Inc.

Manufactured in the United States of America

7   9   10   8

Library of Congress Cataloging-in-Publication Data
Bonhoeffer, Dietrich, 1906–1945.
Creation and fall ; Temptation : two biblical studies /
Dietrich Bonhoeffer.—1st Touchstone ed.
        p.   cm.
First work previously published: c1959.
2nd work previously published: c1955.
Includes bibliographical references and index.
  1. Bible. O.T. Genesis I–IV, 1—Criticism, interpretation, etc.
2. Temptation.   I. Bonhoeffer, Dietrich, 1906–1945. Versuchung.
English.   II. Title: Temptation.
            BS1235.2.B57   1997
    222′.1106—dc21   96-47034   CIP
        ISBN: 978-0-684-82587-8

CREATION AND FALL, translated from SCHÖPFUNG UND FALL,
published by Chr. Kaiser Verlag, Munich, 1937. Translation by
John C. Fletcher, revised by the editorial staff of the SCM Press.

TEMPTATION, VERSUCHUNG, edited by Eberhard Bethge,
first published by Chr. Kaiser Verlag, Munich, 1953,
English translation by Kathleen Downham.

CONTENTS

Creation and Fall

Temptation

Creation and Fall

AUTHOR'S FOREWORD TO GERMAN EDITION

These lectures were delivered in the Winter semester 1932-33 at the University of Berlin and are now made public at the request of those who heard them.

TRANSLATOR'S NOTE

Biblical passages quoted throughout this translation are taken from the Revised Standard Version, by permission of the publishers.

The Church of Christ bears witness to the end of all things. It lives from the end, it thinks from the end, it acts from the end, it proclaims its message from the end. "Remember not the former things, nor consider the things of old. Behold, I am doing a new thing" (Isa. 43.18-19). The new is the real end of the old; Christ is the new. Christ is the end of the old. He is not a continuation of the old; he is not its aiming point, nor is he a consummation upon the line of the old; he is the end and therefore the new.

Within the old world the Church speaks of the new world. And because the Church is more certain of the new world than of anything else it recognizes the old world only in the light of the new. The old world cannot take pleasure in the Church because the Church speaks of its end as though it had already happened—as though the world had already been judged. The old world does not like being regarded as dead. The Church has never been surprised at this, nor is it surprised by the fact that again and again men come to it who think the thoughts of the old world—and who is there entirely free from them? But the Church is naturally in tumult when these children of the world that has passed away lay claim to the Church, to the new, for themselves. They want the new and only know the old. And thus they deny Christ the Lord. Yet the Church, which knows of the end, knows also of the beginning. It knows that there is the same breach between the beginning and now as between now and the end. It knows that the beginning and now are related as life is to death, as the new is to the old. Therefore the Church only sees the beginning in the end; from the end. It sees the creation *sub specie Christi;* better still, in the fallen, old world it believes in the new creation world of the beginning and of the end, because it believes in Christ and in nothing else.

The Church does all this because it is grounded upon the testimony of Holy Scripture. The Church of Holy Scripture —and there is no other "Church"—lives from the end. Therefore it reads all Holy Scripture as the book of the end, of the new, of Christ. What does Holy Scripture, upon which the Church of Christ is grounded, have to say of the creation and the beginning except that only from Christ can we know what the beginning is? The Bible is nothing but the book upon which the Church stands. This is its essential nature, or it is nothing. Therefore the Scriptures need to be read and proclaimed wholly from the viewpoint of the end. Thus the creation story should be read in church in the first place only from Christ, and not until then as leading to Christ. We can read towards Christ only if we know that Christ is the beginning, the new and the end of our world.

Theological interpretation accepts the Bible as the book of the Church and interprets it as such. Its method is this assumption; it continually refers back from the text (which has to be ascertained with all the methods of philological and historical research) to this supposition. That is the objectivity of the method of theological interpretation. And in this objectivity alone is substantiated its claim to a scientific method. When Genesis says "Yahweh," historically or psychologically it means nothing but Yahweh. Theologically, however, i.e. from the Church's point of view, it is speaking of God. God is the One God in the whole of Holy Scripture: the Church and theological study stand and fall with this faith.

I.

THE BEGINNING

1.1-2 In the beginning God created the heavens and the earth. The earth was without form and void, and darkness was upon the face of the deep; and the Spirit of God was moving over the face of the waters.

The Bible begins in a place where our thinking is at its most passionate. Like huge breakers it surges up, is thrown back upon itself and spends its strength. Hardly has the first word of the Bible been visible to us for a moment when it is as though the waves are racing forward again and submerging it with foaming water. That the Bible should speak of the beginning provokes the world and irritates us. For we cannot speak of the beginning; where the beginning begins our thinking stops, it comes to an end. And yet the fact that we ask about the beginning is the innermost impulse of our thinking; for in the last resort it is this that gives validity to every true question we ask. We know that we must not cease to ask about the beginning though we know that we can never ask about it.

Why not? Because we can conceive of the beginning only as something temporal, therefore precisely as that which has no beginning. Because the beginning is freedom and we can conceive of freedom only in terms of necessity—as one thing among others, but never, simply, as the one thing before all others. If we ask why we always think from the viewpoint of the beginning and towards it, and why we can yet never conceive it nor even once get to it by asking, then this question is only the expression of a series of questions which could be pushed back into the infinite and which still did not reach the beginning. Thinking cannot answer its own last "why," because an answer would again produce a "why." The "why" is much more the expression for the beginning-less thinking, *par excellence.*[1] Our thinking, that is, the thinking of those who must go to Christ to know of God, the thinking of fallen man, has no beginning because it is a circle. We think in a circle. We feel and will in a circle. We exist in a circle. We might then say that in that case there is beginning everywhere. We could equally well say that there is no beginning at all: the decisive point is that thinking takes this circle for the infinite and original reality and entangles itself in a vicious circle. For where thinking directs itself upon itself as the original reality it sets itself up as an object, as an object of itself, and therefore it withdraws behind this object again and again—or rather, thinking is antecedent to the object which it sets up. Therefore it is impossible for thinking to make this last predicate about the beginning. In thinking of the beginning thinking collapses. Because thinking desires to penetrate to the beginning and cannot do so, all thinking crumbles into dust, it runs aground upon itself, it breaks to pieces, it is dissolved in the presence of the beginning which thinking posits and cannot posit. The Hegelian question of how to gain a beginning in philosophy is therefore answered only by arbitrarily enthroning Reason in the place of God.

Critical philosophy is therefore systematic despair of its own beginning and of every beginning. Whether critical philosophy proudly renounces that which is not in its power to obtain or whether its resignation leads to its complete destruction, it is always the same human hatred of the beginning, of which we have no knowledge. Man no longer lives in the beginning—he has lost the beginning. Now he finds he is in the middle, knowing neither the end nor the beginning, and yet knowing that he is in the middle, coming from the

---

[1] The German has the Greek phrase κατ' ἐξοχήν. [Tr.]

beginning and going towards the end. He sees that his life is determined by these two facets, of which he knows only that he does not know them. The animals do not know about the beginning and the end; therefore they know no hatred and no pride. Man, aware of being totally deprived of his self-determination—because he comes from the beginning and is moving towards the end without knowing what this means —hates the beginning and rises up against it in pride.

There can therefore be nothing more disturbing or agitating for man than to hear someone speak of the beginning as though it were not the totally ineffable, unutterably dark beyond of our blind existence. We will fall upon him, we will call him an arch-liar or even a saviour, and we will kill him when we hear what he says. Who can say it? Either the one who was a liar from the beginning; the evil one, for whom the beginning is the lie and the lie the beginning, whom man believes because he deceives man. And because he lies he will say: "I am the beginning and you, man, are the beginning. You were with me from the beginning. I have made you what you are and with me is your end. I am the beginning and the end, the Alpha and the Omega; worship me. I am the truth from which the lie comes: for I am the lie that only then gives birth to the truth. You are the beginning and you are the end, for you are in me. Believe in me. I have lied from the beginning; lie, and thus you will be in the beginning and a lord of the truth. Discover your beginning yourself." Thus speaks the evil one, because he has lied from the beginning. Either he is speaking, or the other One who, from the beginning, was the way, the truth and the life, who was in the beginning: God himself, Christ, the Holy Spirit. No one can speak of the beginning but the one who was in the beginning.

Thus the Bible begins with God's free affirmation, free acknowledgment, free revelation of himself: *In the beginning God created.* . . . But the rock in the sea is hardly visible before it is covered again by the sea brought to turmoil by the vision of him who is unshakable. What does it mean that in the beginning is God? Which God? Your God, whom you yourself create out of your need because you need an idol, because you do not wish to live without the beginning or without the end, because you are afraid of being in the middle? In the beginning, God—that is just your lie, which is not better, but more cowardly even than the lie of the evil one. How do you know of the beginning, stranger, you who write this sentence? Have you seen it, were you there in the beginning? Does not your God himself say to you, "Where were you when I laid the foundation of the earth? Answer, if you have understanding" (Job 38.4). What are these first words of Scripture? A delusion of the cowardly imagination of a man who is not able to live in the middle with pride or resignation? Is it the imagination of a man like ourselves when, out of the cowardice of our beginningless and endless lives we cry out to a God who is but our own ego? How shall we be able to answer this reproach? It is true that anyone who speaks of the beginning speaks of his fear within the circle of life, even he who wrote the Bible, he does not speak but God himself speaks, the true primal reality, who was before our life, before our thinking and its fear, who says only of himself that he is in the beginning. He bears witness to himself by nothing but this Word, the word of a book which as the word of a holy man is of itself a word "from the middle" and not "from the beginning." *In the beginning God created* . . . This, said and heard as human word, is the form of the servant in which God encounters us from the beginning and in which alone he is to be found. It is neither profound nor frivolous. It is God's truth, in so far as *he* says it.

In the beginning—God. That is true if he is present to us in the middle with this word as the one who creates and not as one who is remote, reposing, eternally being. We can only *know* of the beginning in the true sense as we hear of it in the middle between beginning and end. Otherwise it would not be *the* beginning which is also our beginning. Of God as the beginning we know here in the middle, between the lost beginning and lost end only—as of the Creator.

In the beginning God *created* the heavens and the earth.

It does not say that first he was and then he created, but that in the beginning God created. This beginning is the beginning in the anxious middle[1] and at the same time beyond the anxious middle where we have our being. We do not know of this beginning by stepping out of the middle and being in the beginning ourselves. Only the lie could give us the power to do this, and therefore we would not be in the beginning but only in the middle and engulfed in the lie. We must bear in mind very clearly that we hear of the beginning only in the middle.

The twofold question arises: Is this beginning God's beginning or is it God's beginning with the world? But the fact that this question is asked is proof that we no longer know what "beginning" means. The beginning can only be spoken of by those who are in the middle and are anxious about the beginning and end, by those who are tearing at their chains, by those—to anticipate something we shall discuss later—who only in their sin know that they are created by God. If this is so we can no longer ask whether this is God's beginning or God's beginning with the world. Luther was once asked what God was doing before the creation of the world. His answer was that he was cutting canes for people who ask such useless questions. This not only stopped the questioner short but also implied that where God is not recognized as the merciful Creator he must needs be known only as the wrathful judge, i.e. always in relation to the situation of the middle, between beginning and end. There is no possible question which could go back beyond this "middle" to the beginning, to God as Creator. Thus it is impossible to ask why the world was created, about God's plan or about the necessity of creation. These questions are finally answered and disposed of as godless questions by the sentence, *In the beginning God created the heavens and the earth.* Not "in the beginning God had this or that idea about the purpose of the world which we

[1] The German has "in der ängstenden Mitte"—"in the anxious-making middle." [Tr.]

now only have to explore further," but "In the beginning God *created.*" No question can penetrate behind God creating, because it is impossible to go behind the beginning.

From there it follows that the beginning is not a temporal distinction. We can always go behind the temporal beginning. But it is the truly unique thing that qualifies the beginning, not quantitatively but in a qualitative sense as something which simply cannot be repeated, which is completely free. We could conceive of a constant repetition of free acts, but this would be basically wrong because freedom does not repeat itself. If it did it would be freedom conditioned by freedom, in other words not freedom, and no longer the beginning.

This quite unrepeatable, unique, free event in the beginning, which must not be confused in any way with the year 4004 or any similar particular date, is the creation. *In the beginning God created the heavens and the earth.* That means that the Creator, in freedom, creates the creature. Their connexion is not conditioned by anything except freedom, which means that it is unconditioned. Hence every use of a causal category for understanding the act of creation is ruled out. Creator and creature cannot be said to have a relation of cause and effect, for between Creator and creature there is neither a law of motive nor a law of effect nor anything else. Between Creator and creature there is simply nothing: the void. For freedom happens in and through the void. There is no necessity that can be shown in God which can or must ensue in creation. There is nothing that causes him to create. Creation comes out of this void.

Now man could certainly once more attempt to move away from the anxiety caused by being in the middle and himself come to be of the beginning. He could attempt to think of this void as the thing which brings forth creation. But where *creation* is talked about, i.e. in theology, the void, the "nothing" has a totally different meaning from when it appears in thinking that has no beginning as the endless end. The void, nothingness, arises in our philosophical thinking where it is impossible to think of the beginning. Then it is ultimately never anything except the ground for being. The void as the ground for being is understood as the creative void: now we would have to take the question back beyond this void without reaching the beginning. The "nothingness" of the man in the middle, who does not know of the beginning, is the last attempt at explanation; it is the point of passage for what is. We call it the void which is brought to consummation, filled to the full and sovereign. The void between God's freedom and the creation is not an attempt to explain what is; it is thus not the matter out of which the world has then paradoxically come into being, the necessary point where what is comes through. Nor is it a thing, not even a negative thing. It is the definition which alone can express the relation of God's freedom to his creation. The void is therefore not a primal possibility, a ground for God himself. It is absolutely nothing; it occurs, rather in the action of God himself, and it always occurs as something already negated, no longer as the void which is happening, but rather as the void which has already happened. We call it the obedient void, the void that waits on God, the void whose glory and existence are neither in itself nor in its nothingness, but only in God's action. Thus God needed no link between himself and the creation. The void is no such "in between"; on the contrary, God only affirms it to the extent that he has overcome it. This is what the Fathers intended to express with the somewhat awkward description of the void as the *nihil negativum* (as opposed to the *nihil privativum,* which was understood to be primal being). The void contains no anxiety for the first creation. On the contrary, it is itself the eternal song praising the Creator who created the world out of nothing. The world stands in the void. This means that it stands in the beginning; and that means nothing except that it is rooted in the freedom of God. The creature belongs to the Creator.

But the God of the creation and of the real beginning is, at the same time, the God of the resurrection. From the beginning the world is placed in the sign of the resurrection of Christ from the dead. Indeed it is because we know of the resurrection that we know of God's creation in the beginning, of God's creation out of nothing. The dead Jesus Christ of Good Friday—and the resurrected Κύριος (Lord) of Easter Sunday: that is creation out of nothing, creation from the beginning. The fact that Christ was dead did not mean the possibility of the resurrection, but its impossibility; it was the void itself, it was the *nihil negativum.* There is absolutely no transition or continuity between the dead and the resurrected Christ except the freedom of God which, in the beginning, created his work out of nothing. If it were possible to intensify the *nihil negativum* we would have to say here of the resurrection that with the death of Christ on the Cross the *nihil negativum* was taken into God himself. "O great affliction, God himself is dead"—but he who is the beginning lived, destroyed the void and created the new creation in his resurrection. By his resurrection we know of the creation— for if he were not resurrected the Creator would be lifeless and would not bear witness to himself. But by his creation we know once more of the power of his resurrection, because he remains the Lord.

In the beginning, out of freedom, out of nothing, God created the heavens and the earth. That is the comfort with which the Bible addresses us who are in the middle, who are anxious before the false void, the beginning without a beginning and the end without an end. It is the gospel, it is the resurrected Christ of whom one is speaking here. God is in the beginning and he will be in the end. He is free regarding the world. The fact that he lets us know this is mercy, grace, forgiveness and comfort.

◆ ◆ ◆

The earth was without form and void, and darkness was upon the face of the deep; and the Spirit of God was moving over the face of the waters.

The beginning has been made. But still our view remains focused upon one event, on the free God. It is true that it is done, that heaven and earth are there. The miracle has come to pass, and it is this that deserves all the wonder. Not the work, no, it is the Creator who is to be glorified. The earth is without form and void, but he is the Lord, who performs the totally new, strange, unfathomable work of his dominion and love. *The earth was without form and void,* nevertheless it was our earth, which has proceeded from God's hand and now lies ready for him, submissive to him in holy worship. God is worshipped first by the earth which was without form and void. He does not need us men to prepare his glory; he creates worship himself from the silent world which slumbers, resting mute and formless in his will.

◆ ◆ ◆

And darkness was upon the face of the deep; and the Spirit of God was moving over the face of the waters.

Considering the action, what can be said about the work? What can be said about the creature, considering the Creator, except that it is dark and in the deep? It is his work, and that is his honour. It is dark before him, and that is the fame of his glory as Creator. His work is beneath him in the deep. Just as we look down, dizzy, from a high mountain into a chasm and the night of the abyss lies beneath us, so is the earth under his feet: distant, strange, dark, deep, but his work.

The dark deep. That is the first sound of the power of darkness, of the Passion of Jesus Christ. The darkness, the *tehom,* the *tihamat,* the Babylonian "primaeval sea" contains within itself, within its depths, power and force. Power and force which now still serve the honour of the Creator, but which once torn away from the origin, from the beginning, are tumult and rebellion. The desolate, empty, dark deep which cannot help itself to form, the conglomeration of the formless, the dull unconscious, the unformed—for in the night, in the abyss, there is only the formless—is both the expression of real submissiveness and the unanticipated force of the formless, which waits for its tying down in form.

It is a moment in God in which the unformed and its Creator are confronted with each other. It is a moment of which it is said that *the Spirit of God was moving over the face of the waters,* it is the moment when God is thinking, planning, engendering *form.* It cannot be said that the relation of Creator and creature is affected in any way, that here

God espouses his creature in order to make it fruitful, that he becomes one with it. The cosmogonic conception of the world-egg over which God broods is not implied here, at any rate. God remains the Creator *over* the deep, *over* the waters. But this God, who is the Creator, now begins again. The creation of the formless, the void and the darkness is distinguished from the creation of form by a movement of God which is characterized here by the movement of the Spirit over the waters. God reflects upon the work. The simultaneous release and joining of formless force into form, of existence into formed being, is the moment of the hesitation of God. The praise which God prepares out of the crude darkness of the unformed shall be completed through the form.

Still the creation is in his hand and power, it has no being of its own. The praise of the Creator is only completed when the creature receives its own being from God and when it praises God's being by having its own being. In the creation of form the Creator renounces himself, since he gives form to his work, since he gives it actual being before himself— but he glorifies himself since this being serves him. With this he immeasurably increases the power of the creation, for he gives to creation actual being in form. This means that creation faces God in a new way, and in thus being over against God the creation belongs entirely to him.

II

THE WORD

1.3 And God said, "Let there be light"; and there was light.

There are myths of creation in which the deity sacrifices its nature, in which the world springs from the natural fruitfulness of the deity, in which creation is conceived as a self-expanding, self-forming birth of the deity, in which the creation itself is a fragment of the nature of God, in which the pangs of nature, its birth and passing away are the pangs of the deity too. In contrast to all this the God of the Bible remains totally God, wholly Creator, completely the Lord, and his creature remains totally the submissive, obedient creature, praising and worshipping him as the Lord. He is never the creation. He is always the Creator. He is not the substance of nature; there is no continuum that binds or unites him with his work. There is only his *Word*.

"God said . . ." The only continuity between God and his work is the Word. That is, "in itself" there is no continuum; if the Word is not there, the world plunges into the bottomless abyss. This Word of God is neither his nature nor his essence but his commandment. It is God himself who thinks and creates in this Word, but God as the one who wills to encounter the creature as Creator. God's creatorhood is neither his nature nor his essence. It is his will and command-

ment in which he gives himself to us as he wills. That God
creates in the Word means that creation is God's command
and order and that this command is free. God *speaks;* this
means that he creates in freedom and in his creating remains
totally free vis-à-vis his work. He is not bound to the work,
but he binds the work to himself. He does not enter into his
work in substance, but his relation to his work is his command. That is, God is never in the world in any way except
in his absolute transcendence of it. He is in the world as
Word, because he is the really transcendent, and he is the
really transcendent because he is in the world *in the Word.*
Only in the Word of creation do we know the Creator, in the
Word in the middle do we have the beginning. Therefore we
do not recognize the Creator "from" his works, as though
the substance, nature or essence of the work were after all
somehow identical with the nature of God, as if there were
perhaps some kind of continuum—perhaps that of cause and
effect. We recognize the Creator only because by his Word
God acknowledges these works and we believe this Word
about these works. Therefore we believe in him as the Creator. It is not a *via eminentiae, negationis, causalitatis!*

God speaks. This must first of all be understood in its
fullest sense. "Word" means "spoken word"—not "symbol"
"meaning" or "idea," but the concrete thing itself. That God,
speaking, creates means that the idea, the name and the work
are one in the created reality in God. The essential point is
therefore not that the Word has "effects" but that God's Word
is itself work. That which in us breaks hopelessly asunder is
for God indissolubly one: the word of command and the
event. With God the imperative is the indicative. The latter
does not follow from the former. The indicative is not the
effect of the imperative; it *is* the imperative. We cannot describe God's creating as an "effect" either, because his Word
does not contain the character of command, the absolute
freedom of creating which comes to expression in the Word
that encompasses a definite reality—the freedom of the Creator from the creature. The "Word" expresses the fact that it
is done out of freedom, the event expresses the fact that it is

done from authority. The fact that it is absolutely impossible for us to think the indicative and the imperative at one and the same time indicates the fact that we no longer live in the unity of the active Word of God, that we are fallen. For us the connexion of imperative and indicative is only conceivable when they are mediated by a continuum, mostly under the scheme of cause and effect. This scheme then attributes the end of the "effect" to the "cause." But this is just what does not apply to the creation. Creation is not an "effect" of the Creator whence we could derive a necessary connection with the cause (Creator). It is a work created in freedom in the Word.

That God speaks and, speaking, creates, the Bible strangely only mentions first where it is concerned with the creation of form, the wresting of form out of the formless. Form corresponds to the Word. The Word moves out forming, and limiting the individual, the real, the whole. The Word calls being out of non-being, so that it may be. It is an absolutely dark, completely inaccessible background that opens here behind the Word of creation. It is simply impossible for us to grasp that first, wordless act of creation, because the Creator is One, and we, as his creatures, are created by his Word. These two moments in God are one act; we cannot express this differently.

Let there be light; and there was light. Because it was dark upon the formless deep, the light must create form. As the formless night becomes form by the light of morning, as the light creates and unveils form, so that primaeval light had to order the chaos, create and unveil form. If that word from the darkness upon the deep was the first reference to the Passion of Jesus Christ, so now the freeing of the submissive, formless deep for its own being by means of the light is the reference to the light that shines in the darkness. The light awakens the darkness to its own being, to free worship of the Creator. Without the light we would not be, for without the light things cannot be "over against" each other, because there is no form. The submissive deep praises God in subjugated, dull, restricted unoppositeness. Form in the light perceives this being over against as its own being, and gives thanks to the Creator alone. The transparency, distinctness, and unburdened state of actual being, contributed by light, in its confrontation with the other created forms and with the Creator, is the work of the first Word of the Creator. In his created light the creation sees his light.

III.

GOD SEES

1.4a And God saw that the light was good.

This is the third moment in God: he views his created work. Like the other two, this moment is not to be thought of in separation from the others. God views his work and is satisfied with it; this means that God loves his work and therefore wills to preserve it. Creation and preservation are two aspects of the one activity of God. It cannot be otherwise than that God's work is good, that he does not reject or destroy but loves and preserves it. God sees his work; comes to rest; he sees that it is good. God's seeing protects the world from falling back into the void, protects it from total destruction. God sees the world as good, as created—even where it is the fallen world—and because of the way God sees his work and embraces it and does not forsake it, we live. That God's work is good in no way means that the world is the best of all conceivable worlds. It means that the world lives completely in the presence of God, that it begins and ends in him and that he is its Lord. Here is meant the goodness which is undifferentiated from evil whose goodness consists in its being under the dominion of God. Thus it is the work itself that is good; the creation is the good work of God which he does for himself. That the work and not only the will is good and intended to be so is biblical as opposed to Kantian understanding. It is the theme of the whole Bible that the thing done, the condition, the embodiment of the will should become deed, that the world is good, that God's kingdom is to be upon the earth, that his will be done on earth. Because the world is God's world it is good. God, who is the Creator and Lord of the world, wills a good world, a good work. The escape from the created work into bodiless spirit, into mind, is forbidden. God wills to look upon his work, to love it, to call it good and preserve it.

There is an essential difference between *creatio continua* (continual creation) and preservation. In the concept of continual creation the world is wrested for ever from the void. But this idea, by the concept of a discontinuous continuity, deprives the creatorhood of God of its absolute freedom and uniqueness. It is just the fact that we cannot anticipate God's action that this idea does not respect. But at the same time the concept of continual creation ignores the reality of the fallen world, which is not ever newly created but *creation preserved*. That God preserves the created world is the judgment which takes the present moment in its reality from God. It means that the world "once" wrested from the void will be preserved in its being. That which is created by the Word out of nothing, that which is called forth into being, remains sustained by the sight of God. It does not sink back again into the moment of becoming, God sees that it is good and his eye resting upon the work preserves the work in being. Therefore the world is preserved only by the one who is its Creator and alone for the one who is its Creator. The world is preserved not for its own sake but for the sake of the sight of God. But the preserved work is still the good work of God.

Creation means wresting out of non-being; *preservation* means confirmation of being. *Creation* is real *beginning*, always "before" my knowledge and before *preservation*. At this point creation and preservation are still one, for they are related to the same object, the original good work of God. Preservation is always "in relation to" creation, and creation is in itself. But the preservation of the original creation and the preservation of the fallen creation are two entirely different things.

IV

THE DAY

1.4b-5 And God separated the light from the darkness.
God called the light Day, and the darkness he called
Night. And there was evening and there was morning,
one day.

The day is the first finished work of God. In the beginning
God created the day. The day bears all other things, and the
world lives amid the changes of the day. The day possesses
its own being, form and power. It is not the rotation of the
earth around the sun—which can be understood physically
—or the calculable change of light and darkness; the day
is something exceeding all this, something determining the
essence of our world and of our existence. If it were not such
an unsuitable thing to say in this context, we might say that it
is what is called a mythological quantity. The gods of day and
night who, according to pagan belief, inspire and animate the
world are here totally dethroned. Nevertheless the world
remains God's first creature, both wondrous and powerful in
the hand of God.

For us the creatureliness and miraculousness of the day
has completely disappeared. We have deprived the day of its
power. We no longer allow ourselves to be determined by the
day. We count and compute it, we do not allow the day to
give to us. Thus we do not live it. Today less than ever—for
technology is a campaign against the day. The Bible too
speaks of the day in the same calculating way as we speak of

it but the Bible knows too that the day is not this calculable day of the earth's rotation—that it is the great rhythm, the natural dialectic of creation. In the morning the unformed becomes form and then by evening sinks back into formlessness. The bright polarity of light dissolves into unity with the darkness. Living sound grows silent in the stillness of the night. An expectant awakening in light follows sleep. There are times (which go far beyond the physical day) of awakening and slumbering in nature, in history, and in nations. All this is what the Bible means when it speaks of the creation of the day, of the day without man, which bears everything, including the lot of man. The rhythm—repose and movement in one—which gives and takes and gives again and takes again, which thus eternally points towards God's giving and taking, to God's freedom on the other side of repose and movement—that rhythm is the day. When the Bible speaks of six days of creation it may well have been thinking of the day of morning and evening, but in any case it does not mean this day in a computable sense; it thinks of it in terms of the power of the day which first makes the physical day what it really is, the natural dialectic of creation. The physical problem does not at all belong to the discussion in which the "day" is being considered. It does not disparage biblical thought, whether the creation occurred in rhythms of millions of years or single days, and we have no occasion to protest the latter or to doubt the former. But the question as such does not concern us. To the extent that his word is the word of man the biblical author was limited by his time and his knowledge, and we dispute this as little as the fact that through this word only God himself is speaking to us of his creation. The days God created are the rhythms in which the creation rests.

V.

THE FIXED

1.6-10 And God said, "Let there be a firmament in the midst of the waters, and let it separate the waters from the waters." And God made the firmament and separated the waters which were under the firmament from the waters which were above the firmament. And it was so. And God called the firmament Heaven. And there was evening and there was morning, a second day. And God said, "Let the waters under the heavens be gathered together into one place, and let the dry land appear." And it was so. God called the dry land Earth, and the waters that were gathered together he called Seas. And God saw that it was good.

Here we have before us the ancient world picture it in all its scientific *naïveté*. While it would not be advisable to be too mocking and self-assured, in view of the rapid changes in our own knowledge of nature, undoubtedly in this passage the biblical author stands exposed with all the limitations caused by the age in which he lived. The heavens and the seas were not formed in the way he says: we would not escape a very bad conscience if we committed ourselves to any such statement. The idea of verbal inspiration will not do. The writer of the first chapter of Genesis is behaving in a very human way. Considering all this there is apparently very little to say about this section. And yet something completely new occurs on this next day of creation. The world of the fixed, the firm, the unchangeable, the unliving comes into being.

It is characteristic that those works of creation which are most distant and strange to us in their fixedness, immutability and repose, were created in the beginning. Unaffected by human life the fixed world stands before God, unchangeable and undisturbed. An eternal law binds it. This law is nothing but the command of the Word of God itself.

The world of the stars belongs to the firmament of the heavens. Therefore let us anticipate here:

1.14-19 And God said, "Let there be lights in the firmament of the heavens to separate the day from the night; and let them be for signs and for seasons and for days and years and let them be lights in the firmament of the heavens to give light upon the earth." And it was so. And God made the two great lights, the greater light to rule the day and the lesser light to rule the night; he made the stars also. And God set them in the firmament of the heavens to give light upon the earth, to rule over the day and over the night, and to separate the light from the darkness. And God saw that it was good. And there was evening and there was morning, a fourth day.

In accordance with eternal, unchangeable laws the days, years and seasons come into being in the firmament. Here number rules and its inflexible law. What does it have to do with our existence? Nothing—the stars go their way, whether man is suffering, guilty or happy. And in their fixedness they praise the Creator. The stars do not look down upon man, they do not accuse, nor do they comfort. They are totally themselves in unapproachable remoteness. They shine by day and by night, but they do it without concern for us. The stars do not take part in man's existence.

However, man participates in the world of the fixed. For he knows *number.* Given to men in the middle is the knowledge of number, of the immutable and the fixed which is apparently not involved in his fall. It is peculiar to man to know that the higher he can rise in the world of number the more rarefied the air is around him; it becomes more restricted, and thinner, so that he cannot live in this world. It is the great temptation of the man who can count, to want to seek comfort in the world of the fixed and to escape into the world which is not concerned with his existence. He does this without recognizing that this very world was there before the world of man came into being, and that it takes no part in the life of man. Why not? Because although man knows number and its secret he no longer knows that even number, which determines days, years and seasons, is not self-contained, that it too rests only upon the Word and command of God.

Number is not itself the truth of God. Like everything else it is his creature and it receives its truth from the Creator. We have forgotten this connexion. When we have number we believe we have truth and eternity. We become aware of this loss when we realize that mathematics too in the last resort does not transcend the world of the paradox. The end of godless calculation is in paradox, in contradiction. So it is for us. In the middle we hear of the world's beginning, as also in the middle we know of the fixed and of number, and not otherwise. But just in this way the world of the fixed is revealed to us anew in its essential being. Because we no longer understand number in its primary meaning we no longer understand the language of the fixed world. What we comprehend is the godless language we speak ourselves, the language of an eternal law of the world resting in itself, silent about the Creator and boasting about the creature. But when we hear of the Creator who in the beginning created the world we know of the lost connexion and believe in God as the Creator, without grasping how he rules over the world of the fixed, without seeing the world of the fixed, the world of number, in its true creatureliness. So we do not see the world of the fixed, of the unchangeable in its original state—the law has become autonomous—but we believe in God as its Creator.

The development which the formless undergoes in the form of the fixed weakens, and at the same time strengthens, its force. Being in form limits the primal force of the un-formed. But at the same tune this separate being in form means praise growing ever more complete and powerful, praise of the Creator who creates praise out of the rigid being of the fixed world. But it also admits the possibility that where the world has once been separated from its origin, from the Creator, the peculiar being of the fixed, of law and of number, will try to rest upon itself and tear its power away from the Creator. To us in the middle, hearing of this beginning of the fixed, of law and number, is given the knowledge that now, in this age, this fixed world boasts of its own being against God and separates itself from him—by our guilt, through our loss of the beginning. So we no longer see the Creator in the world of the fixed, but we believe in him. We see law and number, though in their detachment from God, and we believe in God *beyond* this created world.

The old rationalistic question still remains about the creation of light on the first day and of the sun on the fourth day. Herder has spoken eloquently of how the biblical author may have had in mind a break of day in which the light breaks forth before the sun. Perhaps he was right. But it must be said that light makes the sun what it is and not the sun the light. The physical explanation of the origin of light is no more than an exhibition of a chain of phenomena whose end is "light." In this explanation the objective fact of light is not explained. It is truer to say that the light makes the sun the sun: that the sun shines because light is intended to exist. The fact that we cannot conceive of uncaused light in no way takes away this connexion. The light *per se* of the creation, the light which lay formless over the formless darkness, is bound to form, to law, to the fixed, to number; but it remains in God, it remains God's creation, and never itself becomes calculable number.

VI.

THE LIVING

1.11-13, 20-25 And God said, "Let the earth put forth vegetation, plants yielding seed, and fruit trees bearing fruit in which is their seed, each according to its kind, upon the earth." And it was so. The earth brought forth vegetation, plants yielding seed according to their own kinds, and trees bearing fruit in which is their seed, each according to its kind. And God saw that it was good. And there was evening and there was morning, a third day. And God said, "Let the waters bring forth swarms of living creatures, and let birds fly above the earth across the firmament of the heavens." So God created the great sea monsters and every living creature that moves, with which the waters swarm, according to their kinds, and every winged bird according to its kind. And God saw that it was good. And God blessed them, saying, "Be fruitful and multiply and fill the waters in the seas, and let birds multiply on the earth." And there was evening and there was morning, a fifth day. And God said, "Let the earth bring forth living creatures according to their kinds; cattle and creeping things and beasts of the earth according to their kinds." And it was so. And God made the beasts of the earth according to their kinds and the cattle according to their kinds, and everything that creeps upon the ground according to its kind. And God saw that it was good.

Like a torrent rushing from the heights to the valley below the creation moves from above down to the final work: first the formless, then form in rhythm; then the second form in law, in number. The creation attains to its own being, more and more, ever clearer in separation from the form of the Creator; and it proclaims his nearness ever more jubilantly. But the being of that which has been created so far is dead.

It does not praise the Creator by the continuation of his work but by itself alone.

Now something totally new occurs, without any continuity with that which has happened before. The Creator wills that his creation itself should affirm and continue his work, he wills that created things should live and create further life. The living differs from the dead by the fact that it can itself create life. This God gives to his work: he calls it to life. And that he does this, and that now the living belongs to him in its own creativity and lives in his obedience—this is the new way in which the Creator glorifies himself in his work. He does not will to be Lord of a dead, eternally unchangeable world subjected to him, he wills to be the Lord of life, in all its infinite forms. Thus at his Word the living and the fruitful break forth out of the dead stone, from the unfruitful earth. It is not an event of evolution from death to life, it is God's command which creates the living out of the dead, which can raise children to Abraham out of these stones, which calls Christ to rise from the dead earth. The earth becomes the mother of the living out of whose dead darkness life from now on shall break forth. The world of plants, yielding seed and bearing fruit comes into being; this means that there comes into being the life whose true nature it is to create further life. Plants yielding seed according to their kind means, in the manifold variety of the living. Not only the earth, but also the unliving sea and the fixed heavens become animated by living things which move about. While the plants adhere to the ground, the animals move about, they have mastery over the ground, they are free to walk about over it, they are not bound to it: fish and birds according to their kind, and cattle and creeping things and wild animals according to their kind yielding their seed, in their fruitfulness. It is not the Creator's own nature which he here instils in what is living and life-creating. The living and creative is not the divine; it is and remains the creaturely, the creation, the work separated from the Creator which the Creator freely commands.

The Lord, in his existence over against the creation, wills

to view his own action in living development; he wills to see
himself in his creation, and his creation is to honour him.
One could think that God had now surrendered the work of
preservation to his creatures themselves, that the world and
nature provided for themselves, and that the fixity of the law
and the fruitfulness of the living together constituted the
powers of the preservation of the world. The clock is wound
up and now runs by itself. But the Bible clearly knows that
in the created world nothing runs "by itself." The law and
life-creating life are, as the work of God, created out of
nothing and stand only in the void; that is, only in the freedom of the Word of God. If God withdrew his Word from
his work it would sink back into nothingness. Therefore the
lawfulness of the course of the world and the aliveness of the
creation are not identifiable with the preserving action of
God; on the contrary, the law and life are alone preserved by
the free Word of God. The law and life are not worthy of
adoration, for they are creatures like all others, but the one
who is worthy is the Lord of the law and the Lord of the
living.

Again and again we read, and our section, too, closes with
the words: *And God saw that it was good.* This signifies two
things for us. God's work is good as the unimpaired form of
the will of God. But it is good only in the way that the
creaturely can be good; because the Creator views it, acknowledges it as his own, and says of it: "It is good." God
views his work, and only this makes the work good. This
means particularly that the work is good only because the
Creator alone is good. The goodness of the work is never in
the work itself, but only in the Creator. The goodness of the
work consists precisely in the fact that it very rigidly points
away from itself towards the Creator alone and to his Word
which is good; therefore that "none is good save one, even
God." In the sense of this word of Jesus the first creation is
"good." If none is good save God, only God will be given the
glory. And in this very thing the goodness—but now the real
goodness—of the creation will consist. It will allow
the Creator to be good as its only Lord, it will receive its

goodness from his Word alone and it will know this Word as its only good. We say the same thing in different words when we say that the real being of the creature, its being creature, is totally taken up into the being of God and is fully obedient to him. The being of the formless, the being of that which is shaped into rhythm; the fixed; and the living, as the ever more intensive enhancement of personal action—all this is still created being. That is, it is obedient being and it never knows of its own personal action except in relation to the Word of God, in relation to the freedom of its creation and preservation.

VII

THE IMAGE OF GOD ON EARTH

1.26f. Then God said, "Let us make man in our image, after our likeness; and let them have dominion over the fish of the sea, and over the birds of the air, and over the cattle, and over all the earth, and over every creeping thing that creeps upon the earth." So God created man in his own image, in the image of God he created him; male and female he created them.

God loves his work, he loves it in its own being, for the creature honours the Creator. But still God does not recognize himself in his work; he sees his work but he does not see himself. "To see oneself" means as it were "to behold one's face in a mirror," "to see oneself in a likeness." How shall this come to pass? God remains totally the Creator. His work lies at his feet. How shall he find himself in his work? The work does not resemble the Creator, it is not his image. It is the form of his command. The decisive point is that the work, at the moment when the Creator has brought it forth, is already torn away from the Creator and strange to him; it is no longer the Creator himself. Even in its aliveness the work is dead, because it is an event that has happened, because, while it comes out of freedom, it is itself not free but determined. Only that which is itself free is not dead, is not strange, is not torn away as an event that has happened. Only in something that is itself free can the One who is free, the Creator, see himself. But how can the creation be free? The creation is fixed, bound in law, determined and not free. If the Creator wills to create his own image, he must create it in freedom; and only this image in freedom would fully praise him and fully proclaim the honour of its Creator.

And now the narrative is about us; it is about the creation of man. The Bible expresses the difference of this act from all God's previous creating by the way in which it introduces it. The Hebrew plural is the way in which it shows the significance and sublimity of the Creator's action. We must observe, too, that God does not simply call man forth out of non-being as he has called forth everything else. We become drawn into God's plan, as it were, and by this we become attentive to the fact that something new, something that has never yet been, something quite extraordinary is about to happen.

Then God said, *"Let us make man in our image, after our likeness."*

Man shall proceed from God as his ultimate, his new work, and as the image of God in his creation. There is no transition here from somewhere or other, there is new creation. This has nothing to do with Darwinism: quite independently of this man remains the new, free, undetermined work of God. We have no wish at all to deny man's connexion with the animal world: on the contrary. But we are very anxious not to lose the peculiar relationship of man and God in the process. In our concern with the origin and nature of man, it is hopeless to attempt to make a gigantic leap back into the world of the lost beginning. It is hopeless to want to know for ourselves what man was originally, to identify here man's ideal with the creational reality of God, not to understand that we can know about the man of the beginning only if we start from Christ. This attempt, as hopeless as it is understandable, has again and again delivered the Church up to free speculation at this dangerous point. Only in the middle, as those who live from Christ, do we know of the beginning.

In man God creates his image on earth. This means that man is like the Creator in that he is free. Actually he is free only by God's creation, by means of the Word of God; he is free for the worship of the Creator. In the language of the

Bible, freedom is not something man has for himself but
something he has for others. No man is free "as such," that
is, in a vacuum, in the way that he may be musical, intelligent
or blind as such. Freedom is not a quality of man, nor is it an
ability, a capacity, a kind of being that somehow flares up in
him. Anyone investigating man to discover freedom finds
nothing of it. Why? because freedom is not a quality which
can be revealed—it is not a possession, a presence, an object,
nor is it a form for existence—but a relationship and nothing
else. In truth, freedom is a relationship between two persons.
Being free means "being free for the other," because the
other has bound me to him. Only in relationship with the
other am I free.

No substantial or individualistic concept of freedom can
conceive of freedom. I have no control over freedom as over
a property. It is simply the event that happens to me through
the other. We can ask how we know this, or whether this is
not just again speculation about the beginning resulting from
being in the middle. The answer is that it is the message of
the gospel that God's freedom has bound us to itself, that his
free grace only becomes real in this relation to us, and that
God does not will to be free for himself but for man. God in
Christ is free for man. Because he does not retain his freedom for himself the concept of freedom only exists for us as
"being free for." For us who live in the middle through Christ
and know our humanity in his resurrection, that God is free
has no meaning except that we are free for God. The freedom
of the Creator is proved by the fact that he allows us to be
free for him, and that means nothing except that he creates
his image on earth. The paradox of created freedom cannot
be eliminated. Indeed it must be made as obvious as possible.
Here created *freedom* means—and it is this that goes beyond
all previous deeds of God, the unique *par excellence*—that
God himself enters into his creation.

Now God does not only command and his Word come to
pass, he himself enters into creation and thus creates freedom. Man differs from the other creatures in that God himself is in him, in that he is God's image in which the free

Creator views himself. The old dogmatists meant this when they spoke of the inherence of the Trinity in Adam. In the free creature the Holy Spirit worships the Creator, uncreated freedom praises itself in created freedom. The creature loves the Creator, because the Creator loves the creature. Created freedom is freedom in the Holy Spirit, but as *created* freedom it is the freedom of *man* himself. How does this created being of free man express itself? In what way does the freedom of the Creator differ from the freedom of the created? How is the created free?

Man is free by the fact that creature is related to creature. Man is free for man, *Male and female he created them.* Man is not alone, he is in duality and it is in this dependence on the other that his creatureliness consists. Man's creatureliness is not a quality, something that exists, something that is, any more than his freedom. It can only be defined in man's being over against the other, with the other and dependent upon the other. The "image . . . after our likeness" is consequently not an *analogia entis* in which man, in his being *per se* and *a se*,[1] is in the likeness of the being of God. There is no such analogy between God and man, if only because God—the only One existing in and for himself in his underived being, yet at the same time existing for his creatures, binding and giving his freedom to man—must not be thought of as being alone, inasmuch as he is the God who in Christ bears witness to his "being for man." The likeness, the analogy of man to God, is not *analogia entis* but *analogia relationis.* This means that even the relation between man and God is not a part of man; it is not a capacity, a possibility, or a structure of his being but a given, set relationship: *justitia passiva.* And in this given relation freedom is given. From this it follows secondly, that this analogy must not be understood as though man in some way had this likeness in his possession, at his disposal. The analogy, the likeness must be understood strictly as follows: the likeness has its likeness *only* from the original. It always refers us only to the original, and is "like"

---

[1] The German reads "an und für sich." [Tr.]

only in this way. *Analogia relationis* is therefore the relation given by God himself and is analogy only in this relation given by God. The relation of creature with creature is a God-given relation because it exists in freedom and freedom originates from God.

Man in duality—man and woman—is brought into the world of the fixed and the living in his likeness to God. And just as his freedom over against man consisted in the fact that he was to be free *for* him, his freedom over against the rest of the created world is to be free *from* it. That means that he is its master, he has command over it, he rules it. And here is the other side of man's created likeness to God. Man is to rule—of course as over God's creation, as one who receives the commission and power of his dominion from God. Being free from created things is not the ideal freedom of the spirit from nature. This freedom of dominion directly includes our tie to the creatures who are ruled. The soil and the animals whose Lord I am are the world in which I live, without which I am not. It is my world, my earth, over which I rule. I am not free from it in the sense that my real being, my spirit requires nothing of nature, foreign to the spirit though it may be. On the contrary, in my total being, in my creatureliness, I belong to this world completely. It bears me, nourishes me, and holds me. But my freedom from it consists in the fact that this world, to which I am bound as a lord to his servant, as the peasant to his soil, is subjected to me, that I am to *rule* over the earth which is and remains my earth, and the more strongly I rule it the more it is *my* earth. It is by no other commissioned authority except that given by the Word of God to man—which thus uniquely binds and sets him over against the other creatures.

This we are told, we who in the middle know nothing of all this any more, to whom all this is pious myth or a lost world. We also try to rule, but it is the same here as on Walpurgis Night: we think we are pushing and we are being pushed. We do not rule, we are ruled. The thing, the world, rules man. Man is a prisoner, a slave of the world, and his rule is illusion. Technology is the power with which the earth grips man and subdues him. And because we rule no more, we lose the ground, and then the earth is no longer *our* earth, and then we become strangers on earth. We do not rule because we do not know the world as God's creation, and because we do not receive our dominion as God-given but grasp it for ourselves. There is no "being-free-from" without "being-free-for." There is no dominion without serving God. With the one, man necessarily loses the other. Without God, without his brother, man loses the earth. In his sentimental backing away from dominion over the earth man has always lost God and his brother. God, our brother, and the earth belong together. But for those who have lost the earth, for us men in the middle, there is no way back to the earth except the way to God and to our brother. From the beginning the way of man to the earth has only been possible as God's way to man. Only where God and man's brother come to man can man find the way back to the earth. Man's being-free-for God and the other person and his being-free-from the creature in his dominion over it is the image of God in the first man.

VIII.

BLESSING AND COMPLETION

*1.28-31 And God blessed them, and God said to them,
"Be fruitful and multiply, and fill the earth and subdue it;
and have dominion over the fish of the sea and over the
birds of the air and over every living thing that moves
upon the earth." And God said, "Behold, I have given you
every plant yielding seed which is upon the face of all the
earth, and every tree with seed in its fruit; you shall have
them for food. And to every beast of the earth, and to
every bird of the air, and to everything that creeps on the
earth, everything that has the breath of life, I have given
every green plant for food." And it was so. And God saw
everything that he had made, and behold, it was very
good. And there was evening and there was morning, a
sixth day.*

The blessing of God upon man is his promise, his certain
promise. Blessing means singling out the blessed. The blessing is laid upon man and remains upon him until it is changed
to a curse. Blessing and curse are burdens which God lays
upon man. They descend from generation to generation,
often misunderstood and uncomprehended. They are something wholly real. They are not magical—to the extent that
this word is connected with enchantment—they are real.
This blessing—*be fruitful and multiply, and fill the earth and
subdue it*—affirms man totally in the world of the living in
which he is placed. It is his total empirical existence that
is blessed here, his creatureliness, his worldliness, and his
earthliness. But what if this blessing is suddenly changed into
a curse? What this blessing signifies above all else is that God
saw that his work was very good. And there was morning and
evening of the sixth, the last day.

PART 2

I.

BLESSING AND COMPLETION *(Continued)*

> 2.1-3 *Thus the heavens and the earth were finished, and all the host of them. And on the seventh day God finished his work which he had done, and he rested on the seventh day from all the work which he had done. So God blessed the seventh day and hallowed it, because on it God rested from all his work which he had done in creation.*

In the Bible "rest" really means more than "having a rest." It means rest after the work is accomplished, it means completion, it means the perfection and peace of God in which the world rests, it means transfiguration, it means turning our eyes absolutely upon God's being God and towards worshipping him. It is never the rest of a lethargic God; it is the rest of the Creator. It is no relinquishing of the world, but the ultimate glorification of the world which is gazing upon the Creator. God must remain the Creator in his rest, too; "my Father worketh hitherto, and I work." God remains the Creator, but now as the one who has accomplished his work. We now understand God's rest to be at the same time the rest of his creation. His rest is our rest (as his freedom is our freedom, his goodness our goodness). Therefore God sanctifies the day of his rest for Adam and for us, whose heart is restless until it finds rest in God's rest. As far as we are concerned this rest is the promise which has been given to the people of God. It is unbelieving insolence either to want to snatch God's peace for ourselves prematurely in pious quietism or to reason impudently about the boredom of the peace of paradise, thereby combining and glorifying unrest and battle.

This loud pleasure in one's own personal vitality might have to grow silent very quickly in the presence of the "living" God.

It is the day which in the New Testament is the day of the Lord's resurrection. It is the day of rest, the day of victory, of dominion, of perfection, of transfiguration; for us, the day of worship, the day of hope looking towards the day of final rest with God, the "rest of the people." All the days of the week have really only been created for its sake. Thou shalt keep holy the holiday and not sleep it away. For the sake of the final rest, for the sake of the resurrection of Jesus Christ, for the sake of the day of the final resurrection and the rest of the Creator with his creatures everything has been created, we have been created "that they may rest from their labours, for their works follow with them."

II.

THE OTHER SIDE

*2.4aff. These are the generations of the heavens and the
earth when they were created.*

Men soon became aware of the fact that here there is a
second creation story essentially older than and totally different from the first. How is this to be judged? What does it
mean for our interpretation? From the first glance at the
whole of both creation stories it is plain that both the ac-
counts are only representations of the one thing from two
sides; it must even be said that the first without the second,
like the second without the first would not express what
ought to be said here. Of course we have only arrived at this
judgment from the Scripture perceived and grasped as a
totality.

The first account is written entirely as from above, from
God's point of view. Here man is the final work of God's
self-glorification. The world is created for God, for his honour
alone, and man is the most precious vessel the mirror of the
Creator himself. It is totally for the sake of God's glory and
honour as Creator that all things come to pass; in spite of the
creation of man the world remains the world in the deep, the
strange, distant world. On the other hand, the second account is about the near world and the near Lord upon the
earth, living together with Adam in *Paradise*. In the first act

count we find man-for-God, here we have God-for-man;
there the Creator and Lord, here the near, the fatherly God.
There we find man as the final work of God, the whole world
created before man, here we find the direct opposite: in the
beginning there is man, and round about man, for the sake
of man, God fashions animals and birds and for him the trees
grow. Here is the story of man, there God's deed. Here is the
story of man with God, there of God's deed with man. Here
there is the near God, there the strange God. Here is God
himself in the form of man: the God of childlike anthropomorphism, there is God in his deity. Yet certainly both are
only human words, childlike but humble words about the
same God and the same man. Gen. 2 is the other side of
Gen. 1, not arbitrary but necessary—at least when the whole
has been understood.

> *2.4bff.* In the day that the Lord God made the earth and
> the heavens, and no plant of the field was yet in the
> earth and no herb of the field had yet sprung up—for
> the Lord God had not caused it to rain upon the earth,
> and there was no man to till the ground; but a mist went
> up from the earth and watered the whole face of the
> ground.

This approximately corresponds to *without form and void* in
the first account.

III.

MAN OF EARTH AND SPIRIT

2.7 Then the Lord God formed man of dust from the ground, and breathed into his nostrils the breath of life; and man became a living being.

With a significance and an exclusiveness totally different from those we have seen hitherto we are here referred to the earth. The thing that is of interest here is not cosmic; it is our earth and man. God too receives his own definite proper name here, Yahweh (about the meaning of which there is disagreement). This is God's real name: this very God who is spoken of here. *Elohim* in Gen. 1 is not a proper but a generic name, therefore perhaps meaning "deity." We could say that the proper name is proof of a very primitive idea of God and shows that we have no right to speak here of the God whose power was mentioned in the first chapter. But we would have to reply to this that anthropomorphism in thinking of God, undisguised mythology, is no more irrelevant or unsuitable as a way of speaking of the being of God than the abstract use of the generic name "deity." On the contrary, the fact that we imply cannot conceive of "God in himself." is perhaps expressed much more plainly in clear anthropomorphism. The abstract concept of God is fundamentally much more anthropomorphic, just because it is not intended to be anthropomorphic, than childlike anthropomorphism. By using a proper name for God we can conceive of God correctly.

Indeed, the proper name is God himself. We do not have
God in any way except in his name. This is true today as well:
"Jesus Christ" is the name of God. This is highly anthropo-
morphic and highly objective at the same time.

♦ ♦ ♦

Then the Lord God formed man of dust from the ground, and
breathed into his nostrils the breath of life.

Here everything takes place in a very earthly way. The
language is extremely childlike, and shocking for those who
want to "understand," to know anything. How can we speak
of God in the way that we speak of a man shaping his vessel
out of earth and clay? The anthropomorphisms become more
intolerable: God forming and shaping the clay, and man
shaped like a vessel out of a clod of earth. This can surely not
produce any knowledge about the origin of man! To be sure,
as a narrative this story is just as irrelevant or meaningful as
any other myth of creation. And yet in its capacity as the
Word of God it is the source of knowledge concerning the
origin of man. And now we shall see that what is narrated
here fits in exactly with the previous narration and forms a
unity with it.

Yahweh shapes man with his own hands. This expresses
two things. First, the bodily nearness of the Creator to the
creature, that it is really he who makes me—man—with his
own hands; his concern, his thought for me, his design for
me, his nearness to me. And secondly there is his authority,
the absolute superiority in which he shapes and creates me,
in which I am his creature; the fatherliness in which he
creates me and in which I worship him. That is God himself,
to whom the whole Bible testifies.

The man whom God has created in his image, that is in
freedom, is the man who is formed out of earth. Darwin and
Feuerbach themselves could not speak any more strongly.
Man's origin is in a piece of earth. His bond with the earth
belongs to his essential being. The "earth is his mother"; he
comes out of her womb. Of course, the ground from which
man is taken is still not the cursed but the blessed ground. It
is God's earth out of which man is taken. From it he has his

body. His body belongs to his essential being. Man's body is not his prison, his shell his exterior, but man himself. Man does not "have" a body; he does not "have" a soul; rather, he "is" body and soul. Man in the beginning is really his body. He is one. He is his body, as Christ is completely his body, as the Church is the body of Christ. The man who renounces his body renounces his existence before God the Creator. The essential point of human existence is its bond with mother earth, its being as body. Man has his existence as existence on earth; he does not come to the earthly world from above, driven and enslaved by a cruel fate. He comes out of the earth in which he slept and was dead; he is called out by the Word of God the Almighty, in himself a piece of earth, but earth called into human being by God. "Awake, thou that sleepest, and arise from the dead, and Christ shall shine upon thee." [1] Michelangelo also meant this. Adam resting on the newly created ground is so closely and intimately bound up with the ground on which he lies that he himself, in his still dreaming existence, is strange and marvellous to the highest degree but just the same he is a piece of earth Surely, it is in this full devotion to the blessed ground of creation's earth that the complete glory of the first man becomes visible. And in this resting on the ground, in this deep sleep of creation, man experiences life through bodily contact with the finger of God—the same hand that has made man touches him tenderly as from afar and awakens him to life. God's hand does not hold man in its embrace any longer, but it sets him free, and its creative power becomes the demanding love of the Creator towards the creature. The hand of God portrayed by the picture in the Sistine Chapel reveals more wisdom about the creation than many a deep speculation.

◆ ◆ ◆

And God breathed into his nostrils the breath of life; and man became a living being.

Here body and life enter into one another totally. God

[1] Eph. 5.14.

breathes his Spirit into the body of man. And this Spirit is life and makes man alive. God creates other life through his Word; where man is concerned he gives of his life, of his Spirit. Man as man does not live without God's Spirit. To live *as man* means to live as body in Spirit. Escape from the body is escape from being man and escape from the spirit as well. Body is the existence-form of spirit, as spirit is the existence-form of body. All this can be said only of man, for only in man do we know of body and spins. The human body is distinguished from all non-human bodies by being the existence-form of God's Spirit on earth, as it is wholly undifferentiated from all other life by being of this earth. The human body really only lives by God's Spirit; this is indeed its essential nature. God glorifies himself in the body: in this specific form of the human body. For this reason God enters into the body again where the original in its created being has been destroyed. He enters it in Jesus Christ. He enters into it where it is broken, in the form of the sacrament of the body and of the blood. The body and blood of the Lord's Supper are the new realities of creation of the promise for the fallen Adam. Adam is created as body, and therefore he is also redeemed as body, in Jesus Christ and in the Sacrament.

Man thus created is man as the image of God. He is the image of God not in spite of but just because of his bodiliness. For in his bodiliness he is related to the earth and to other bodies, he is there for others, he is dependent upon others. In his bodiliness he finds his brother and the earth. As such a creature man of earth and spirit is in the likeness of his Creator, God.

IV.

THE MIDDLE OF THE EARTH

2.8-17 And the Lord God planted a garden in Eden, in
the east; and there he put the man whom he had formed.
And out of the ground the Lord God made to grow every
tree that is pleasant to the sight and good for food, the
tree of life also in the midst of the garden, and the tree of
the knowledge of good and evil. A river flowed out of
Eden to water the garden, and there it divided and
became four rivers. The name of the first is Pishon; it is
the one which flows around the whole land of Havilah,
where there is gold; and the gold of that land is good;
bdellium and onyx stone are there. The name of the
second river is Gihon; it is the one which flows around
the whole land of Cush. And the name of the third river
is Hiddekel, which flows east of Assyria. And the fourth
river is Euphrates. The Lord God took the man and put
him in the garden of Eden to till it and keep it. And the
Lord God commanded the man, saying, "You may freely
eat of every tree of the garden; but of the tree of the
knowledge of good and evil you shall not eat, for in the
day that you eat of it you shall die."

How should we speak of the young earth except in the
language of fairy tales? God prepares an exceedingly beautiful garden for man, whom he has created with his own hands.
And what will the man of the desert think of but a land with
beautiful streams and trees full of fruit? Precious stones, rare
odours, splendid colours surround the first man. Perhaps that
place, that garden of the first man was in the fruitful land in
the distant East, between the Euphrates and the Tigris, of
which so many wonderful things have been said? Who can
speak of these things except in pictures? Pictures are not lies:
they denote things, they let the things that are meant shine
through. But pictures change, of course; the pictures of a

child are different from those of an adult, those of the man
of the desert are different from those of the man of the city.
Either way they remain true, just as human speech and the
expression of ideas generally can remain true. They are true
to the extent that God remains in them.

Entirely within the framework of this picture it is related
how man was put into this garden in order to live in it and
how two trees stood in the middle of the garden: one the tree
of life, the other the tree of the knowledge of good and evil.
And upon these two trees the destiny of man is to be decided.
We remain completely in the world of pictures, in the world
of the magical, of magic effects by means of forbidden con-
tacts with sacred objects. We hear of trees of miraculous
power, of enchanted animals, of fiery angel forms, the ser-
vants of a God who walks in his magic garden, of their mysterious deeds, of the creation of woman from the rib of man—
and in the midst of this world is man, the intelligent, who
knows the world around him, who names it freely, before
whom all the animals appear in order to receive their names.
Man is naked and unashamed. Man, too, speaks and walks
with God as if they belonged to one another. He speaks
with the beasts in the fields and lives in his magic garden
magnificently and in peace—and then he reaches for the
fruit of a magic tree and in that moment loses his paradise.
"A myth, a childlike, fantastic picture of the grey, hidden
times of old": thus speaks the world. "God's Word, even in
the beginning of history, before history, beyond history and
yet in history; *we ourselves* are confronted, intended, addressed, accused, sentenced, expelled. *God himself* is the one
who blesses and curses. It is *our* pre-history, truly our own.
It is the beginning, destiny, guilt and end of every one of us":
thus speaks the Church of Christ.

Why dispute the one at the expense of the other? Why can
we not understand that all our speaking about God, about
our beginning and end, about our guilt, *never* mentions these
things themselves but always speaks only in pictures? Why
can we not understand that God must reach out towards us
with these ancient, magical pictures as well as with our tech-

nical, conceptual pictures, that he must teach us if we are to become wise? What we must do, therefore, when interpreting the following is to translate the old picture language of the world of magic into the new picture language of the technical world. We must always assume that in either case it is we who are aimed at and we must readily and openly allow what was said in that age about the man of the magical world-picture to apply to us. We are certainly different from them in that Christ has appeared, while they waited; but we are the same in that, whether in hope or in fulfilment, we can live only through Christ—as those who were lost and who, in hope or fulfilment, are pardoned.

In the middle of the garden there stand two trees with particular names connecting them with human existence in a particular way: the tree of life and the tree of the knowledge of good and evil. To the latter is attached the prohibition to eat of its fruit: the threat of death. *Life, knowledge* and *death*, these three things are connected here and the point is to grasp this connexion. It seems that historically the stories of the tree of life and of the tree of knowledge originally came from different sources. But that is all very obscure: what we are concerned about is the actual text as the Church of Christ has it today.

First of all there is the tree of life. It follows from the context that man was not expressly forbidden to eat of it. In fact, this tree first gains its proper meaning after man has fallen prey to death by eating of the tree of knowledge. Before this, life was not problematic nor was it something to be pursued or seized. It was there, given, life in the presence of God. For this reason the tree of life is only mentioned very simply in this passage. It was in the middle—that is all that is said about it. The life that comes forth from God is in the middle. This means that God, who gives life, is in the middle. In the middle of the world which is at Adam's disposal and over which he has been given dominion is not Adam himself but the tree of divine life. Adam's life comes from the middle which is not Adam himself but God. It constantly revolves around this middle without ever making the attempt to make this middle of existence its own possession. It is characteristic of man that his life is a constant circling around its middle, but that it never takes possession of it. And this life from the middle, which only God possesses, is undisturbed as long as man does not allow himself to be flung out of his groove. Adam is not tempted to touch the tree of life, to lay violent hands on the divine tree in the middle; there is no need at all to forbid this; he would not understand the prohibition. He has life.

But life is his in a particular way. In the first place, *he* really has it (it does not only have him). Secondly, he has it in the unity of unbroken obedience to the Creator; he has it just because he lives from the middle of life and on the strength of the middle of life but he himself does not live in the middle. The perfect unbrokenness of obedience, i.e. his innocence and his ignorance of disobedience, is the characteristic certainly of Adam's life. The life that God gave to man is not simply a state or a quality of man, it is something which has been given to him only in his whole being as man. He has life from God and in the presence of God. He receives it— not as an animal but as man; he has it in his obedience, in his innocence, in his ignorance; that is, he has it in his freedom. Man lives by reason of obedience issuing from freedom. So while it cannot occur to Adam directly to lay hands on the tree of life, because he has life the tree of life can still be endangered indirectly from elsewhere. It can be endangered by the freedom in the unbroken unity of obedience, in which Adam has life, that is, by the tree of the knowledge of good and evil. *In what way?*

Like the tree of life, the tree of the knowledge of good and evil stands in the middle of the garden. But the reference to it contains a special Word of God: the prohibition to eat of it and the threat of death as soon as man transgresses this commandment. How can Adam grasp what death is, what good and evil are, or even what prohibitions in general are, living as he does in unbroken obedience to the Creator? Can all this mean anything to him except empty words?

Certainly Adam cannot know what death, or good, or evil

are, but Adam understands that in these words God confronts him and points out his limit. We ask, How can Adam, the innocent, who does not know about good or evil, understand the Word of God confronting him as prohibition? Two things are contained in the prohibition. First, there is the reference to Adam's being as man, to his freedom ("for" and "from"). It is Adam, the man, who is addressed, in his being as man; Adam understands this. Secondly, this man, who is addressed as one who is free, is shown his limit, that is to say, his creatureliness. In the prohibition Adam is addressed in his freedom and in his creatureliness, and by the prohibition his being is confirmed in its kind. It means nothing but "Adam, thou art as thou art because of me, thy Creator; so be as thou art. Thou art a free creature, so be a creature." This "so be . . ." is not a second thing apart from the first. It is always included in the first, guaranteed by the first. Adam is addressed in his being as man: this it is that he receives from God on this occasion. This peculiar being together which is in truth the very fusion of freedom and creaturehood, is expressed in the picture language of the Bible by the fact that the tree of knowledge, the forbidden tree that denotes the limit of man, stands in the middle. *Man's limit is in the middle of his existence,* not on the edge. The limit which we look for on the edge is the limit of his condition, of his technology, of his possibilities. The limit in the middle is the limit of his reality, of his true existence. In the knowledge of the limit on the edge there is constantly given the possibility of an inner boundlessness. In the knowledge of the limit in the middle all existence, man's being from every possible standpoint, is limited. By the limit—the tree of knowledge—there is also the tree of life, that is, the life-giving Lord himself. He is at once the limit and the middle of our existence; Adam knows that.

But his knowledge is such that it is only an expression for his being from the middle and directed towards the middle, an expression for his creaturehood and for his freedom. Adam's knowledge is embedded in his freedom for God, in his unbroken obedience to God; it is knowledge issuing from freedom of the creature, knowledge in life, knowledge in ignorance. For this reason Adam cannot know or think evil or death. But he knows his limit because he knows God. He does not know that the limit can be transgressed—if he did he would know about evil—but he knows it as the given grace of his creatureliness and freedom. Further, he knows his life is possible only by his limit; he lives from this limit which is in the middle. Thus he understands the prohibition and the threat of death only as a fresh gift, as the grace of God. The limit is grace because it is the basis of creatureliness and freedom; the limit is the middle. Grace is that which supports man over the abyss of non-being, non-living, that which is not created—and all this nothingness is only conceivable to Adam in the form of the given grace of God. No word in the passage indicates the possibility of understanding the prohibition differently, perhaps as temptation. The prohibition of paradise is *grace* of the Creator towards the creature. God tempts no man. Up to this point only the Creator knows what the tree of the knowledge of good and evil is. Adam does not know it yet. Living in the unity of obedience, he cannot understand that which is twofold; living in the unity of the knowledge of God as the middle and the limit of his life, he cannot think of the breaking asunder of knowledge into good and evil. Adam knows neither what is good nor what is evil; in the most particular sense he lives beyond good and evil. He lives the life that comes from God, in whose presence life in either good or evil would mean the unthinkable fall.

"Good and evil," *tob* and *ra,* here have a much wider meaning than "good" and "evil" in our terminology. "The words *tob* and *ra* speak of an ultimate division in the world of man in general which goes beyond the moral discord, so that *tob* would perhaps also mean 'full of pleasure' and *ra* 'full of pain' " (Hans Schmidt). *Tob* and *ra* are the categories for the deepest division of human life in every aspect. The essential thing about them is that they appear as a pair and that, in their state of division, they belong inseparably together. *Tob,* the pleasureful, the good, the beautiful does not exist without being constantly submerged in *ra,* the painful, evil, mean, impure. And—in this wide sense—the painful, the evil, does not exist without a glimmer of pleasure, which makes pain wholly pain. *Tob,* the good, is for us always only that which has been wrested from evil, which has gone through evil, which has been conceived, carried and borne by evil. The glitter of the good, that which is full of joy and pleasure, is its origin in evil. It is good because it has overcome evil, but in the same way as the child "overcomes" his mother's womb. This means that the good is ennobled by the quantity of evil out of which it has torn itself. To us Ignatius is "greater" than Francis, Augustine is greater than Monica, Hagen is greater than Siegfried. But in the same way "evil" is ennobled by the "good" from which it originates; the pain is ennobled by the pleasure out of whose depth it was alone possible. No real evil totally lacks the glitter of the good. In man the purely evil, the purely painful does not exist. In a case of pure evil, not ennobled by good, where the debased itself takes on form, man has lost his manhood and we say he is ill. It is possible for that which is purely painful to possess man, so that that which is full of pleasure is totally destroyed in the painful. In that case man has the mental illness we call melancholia and there he is no longer man. The healthy man is borne up in pain and nourished by that which is full of pleasure; he is torn in pleasure by pain, in good he is torn by evil, in evil he is torn by good. He is divided.

Thus are we who have eaten of the tree of knowledge, not Adam. But we must go one step further in order to understand fully the Bible story of the tree of knowledge, " . . . *for in the day that you eat of it you shall surely die."* The tree of knowledge is the tree of death. It stands immediately next to the tree of life, and the tree of life is only endangered by the tree of death. Both are still untouched and untouchable, limit and middle. Those who reach out for life must die— "whoever would save his life will lose it." And nobody will reach out for it who has not lost it. But he who has lost his life has won the knowledge of good and evil. He it is who lives in division. Why has he lost life? We have said that what

is pleasureful and good is submerged in that which is painful
and evil, and vice-versa. But exactly what is painful in pleasure? It is that in all pleasure man desires eternity, and that
he knows pleasure is transitory and has an end. This is not a
result of previous knowledge, which is now applied to every
pleasureful event. It reveals to us the depth of pleasure itself
if we listen to it; the thirst, the search for eternity, just because it is not eternal but has fallen into death. And on the
other hand we ask what is the pleasure in pain? It is that man
in the depth of pain feels the pleasure of transitoriness, the
pleasure of the extinction of apparently infinite pain, the
pleasure in death.

What is the evil in good? It is that the good dies. What is
the good in evil? It is that the evil dies. What is the division,
the torn condition of the world and of man in *tob* and *ra?* It
is the dying, in pleasure and pain, of man himself. The man
who knows of *tob* and *ra* at the same moment knows of his
death. Knowing of *tob* and *ra* is itself his death. Man dies of
the knowledge of good and evil. Man is dead in his good and
in his evil. Death as transitoriness is not the death that comes
from God. What does "to be dead" mean? It does not mean
the abolition of created being; it means no longer being able
to live—and yet having to live—in the presence of God. It
means to stand before him outlawed, lost and damned, but
not non-existing. And this means to receive life from God no
longer as grace which comes out of the middle and the limit
of real existence but to receive it as a commandment standing
in the way before me and with a flaming sword blocking
every retreat. In this sense "to be dead" means to have life
not as a gift but as a commandment. No one can evade this
commandment, not even by means of self-chosen death,
since being dead itself is under the commandment of life. To
be dead means to have to live. That irritates our natural
thinking. Being dead is not deliverance, salvation or the final
possibility of escape—on the contrary, flight into death is
flight into the most terrible servitude to life. The inescapabil-
ity of life as commandment—that is the knowledge of death.

In the commandment to live something is demanded of

me which I am not in a position to fulfil. I am to live out of my own self, from my own resources, and I cannot. This is the commandment that burdens the man who knows *tob* and *ra*. He is to live out of his own self and he does, but he cannot. He does it by living out of his inner division, by living out his good from evil and his evil from good, by taking the strength of pain from pleasure and the strength of pleasure from pain. He lives in a circle, he lives out of himself, he is alone. But he cannot, because in fact he is not alive but dead in this life. because he must accomplish it out of his own self and just that is his death—both as the cause of his knowledge and as his real cause. The man who is faced by Gods commandment as demand is thrown back upon himself and must live in this way. Man now lives only out of his own self, out of his knowledge of good and evil, and in this he is dead.

Without elaborating further it is clear that the tree of life is only in danger where the tree of death has had its effect. It is clear why the prohibition was concerned with the tree of death and not with the tree of life, or conversely, why the tree with which the prohibition was concerned had to be the tree of death. But one thing remains which we cannot understand, and that is how the deed was done which opened and created our world of division for us. There is knowledge of the torn world of *tob* and *ra* only in death. And Adam knows nothing of this world. For him it remains veiled in the tempting fruit of the tree of knowledge. He knows that the secret of his limit and of his life is in God's keeping.

But here, too, we must remember that this is not the tale of some original man that leaves us more or less uninvolved. If this were so our task would be to let our imagination play in order to remove ourselves into the fairyland beyond *tob* and *ra*. Every such play of imagination would altogether leave out of account our own situation; such a thing would only be possible in the world of division in which man thinks he can still escape from himself in some way. It depends much more upon knowing that this story challenges us, not as imaginative listeners but as men who, with the utmost endeavour of our imagination and all the other powers of our souls, are simply not in a position to remove ourselves to this paradise "beyond good and evil," beyond pleasure and pain. This story challenges us as men who, with all our thinking, remain fastened to the torn world, to antithesis, to contradiction. This is so because our thinking itself is only the expression of our being, of our existence which is grounded in contradiction. Because our existence is not in unity our thinking is torn apart as well.

But now Adam is put before us. Not to sanction this impossibility, not to judge what the Bible calls good from the point of view of that which we call good, or to criticize from this point of view the biblical discourse beyond good and evil: Adam is put before us to disturb us and to be our critic. This is so just because Adam is a man like us and because his history is our history—with the one decisive difference that for us it begins where it ends for Adam. Our history is history through Christ where Adam's history is history through the serpent. But as those who only live and have a history through Christ, our imagination cannot help us to know about the beginning. We can only know about it from the new middle, from Christ, as those who are freed in faith from the knowledge of good and evil and from death, and who can make Adam's picture their own only in faith.

V.

THE STRENGTH OF THE OTHER PERSON

> *2.18-25 Then the Lord God said, "It is not good that the man should be alone; I will make him a helper fit for him." So out of the ground the Lord God formed every beast of the field and every bird of the air and brought them to the man to see what he would call them; and whatever the man called every living creature, that was its name. The man gave names to all cattle, and to the birds of the air, and to every beast of the field; but for the man there was not found a helper fit for him. So the Lord God caused a deep sleep to fall upon the man, and while he slept took one of his ribs and closed up its place with flesh; and the rib which the Lord God had taken from the man he made into a woman and brought her to the man. Then the man said, "This at last is bone of my bones and flesh of my flesh; she shall be called woman, because she was taken out of man." Therefore a man leaves his father and his mother and cleaves to his wife, and they become one flesh. And the man and his wife were both naked, and were not ashamed.*

It does not seem relevant that the creation of woman is mentioned just here. And from the point of view of the narrative it is undoubtedly wrong that woman has not heard God's prohibition, because this circumstance has no inner meaning at all. Yet this part of the story does have its special significance. Let us bear in mind that the tree of life is mentioned first: as yet no one desires it and no prohibition is attached to it; nevertheless it is the tree whose fruit is ultimately the pivot of everything that happens. We have seen that it was only endangered by the tree of knowledge. Now the series of events which condenses this danger and makes it more and more threatening goes on and on. The tree of knowledge is followed by the creation of woman, and in the end it is the

serpent that leads to the assault on the trees of knowledge
and life. The inconceivability of this act makes the writer,
most profoundly, draw into view and into this context everything that can be thought of to make it more conceivable or
rather, to make its inconceivability clear. It is clear that in the
writer's view the creation of woman is a part of the pre-history
of the Fall of man.

◆ ◆ ◆

*"It is not good that the man should be alone; I will make him
a helper fit for him."*
The first man is alone. Christ was also alone. And we are
alone as well. Everyone is alone in his own way: Adam is
alone in the expectation of the other person, the community.
Christ is alone because only he loves the other person, because he is the way by which mankind has returned to its
Creator. We are alone because we have pushed the other
person from us, because we hated him. Adam was alone in
hope, Christ was alone in the fullness of deity, and we are
alone in evil, in hopelessness.

God creates a companion, a helpmeet, for Adam. It is not
good that Adam is alone. For what purpose does man, living
in the protection of God, need a companion? The answer is
only revealed if we consider the story in its context again and
again. In the Bible otherwise only God is a companion, a
helpmeet to man. So if woman is here spoken of in this way
it must mean something quite unusual. This follows from the
description. First of all God forms animals out of the ground
from which he formed man. According to the Bible men
and animals have the same bodies! Perhaps he may find a
companion among these brothers, for the animals really are
of the same origin as he. The peculiar feature of this is that
man must obviously know for himself whether these animals
can be companions for him or not. Adam's companion was to
be whichever creature he called his companion as the creatures were brought before him. There is Adam, the intelligent, calling all the animals by name—the brotherly world of
the animals who have been taken from the same ground as
he—and letting them pass by him. It was his first pain that

these brothers whom he loved did not fulfil his own expectations: they remained a strange world to him. Indeed, in all good fellowship, they remain creatures subjected to him, whom he names and over which he rules. Adam remains alone. As far as I know, nowhere else in the history of religions have the animals been spoken of in such a significant context. When God desires to create for man, in the form of another creature, the helper he is himself, in the first place the animals are created; they are named and set in their places. Still Adam is alone. That which came out of the ground remains a stranger to him.

Now something strange occurs: Adam must fall into a deep sleep. What man cannot find or do while he is awake God does with him when he is asleep. Adam does not really know how it happens. But he knows that God has used him, that God took a piece of his body while he was asleep and formed the other person from it. It is with a true cry of joy that Adam recognizes the woman: *"This at last is bone of my bones and flesh of my flesh; she shall be called woman, because she was taken out of man."*

Thus Adam knows that this creature, whom God has shaped with his assistance, out of his flesh, is unique, but he sees this action of his upon the other entirely as a gift of God. The fact that Eve derives from him is in Adam's eyes not a cause for glorification but for special gratitude. He does not put forward any claim for himself: he knows that he is connected in a completely new way to this Eve, who derives her existence from him. It is best to describe this unity by saying that now he belongs to her because she belongs to him. They are no longer without one another; they are one and yet two. The fact of two becoming one is itself the mystery which God has established by his action upon the sleeping Adam. They were one from their origin and only when they become one do they return to their origin. This becoming one is never the fusion of the two, the abolition of their creatureliness as individuals. It is the utmost possible realization of their belonging to one another, which is based directly upon the fact that they are different from one another.

In what way is Eve a "helper" to Adam? In the context of
the whole it can only be that woman becomes man's helper
in the carrying of the limit imposed upon him. What does
this mean? Adam was alone. In God's prohibition he was
addressed—as we have seen—in his being as man, in his
freedom and in his creatureliness. He had them, because he
received them in unbroken obedience, in daily converse with
his Creator. He knew he was limited, but only in the positive
sense that to him it was unthinkable to pass the limit. In this
limitation he had his life, it is true, but he could still not
really love this life in its limitation. His life between love and
hate was much more the purely faithful and visible reception
of the divine gift. In his unfathomable mercy the Creator
knew that this creaturely, free life can only be borne in limitation if it is loved, and out of this mercy he created a companion for man who must be at once the embodiment of Adam's
limit and the object of his love. And in fact the love for
woman was not to be the life of man in the truest sense.
Limit and life, these are the untouchable, inaccessible middle
of paradise around which Adam's life revolves. It takes on
form and by the hand of God the Creator it becomes Adam's
companion. There is knowledge of the other person as a
creature of God, and knowledge of the other person as simply
the other person who stands next to me, limiting me; there is
at the same time the knowledge that the other person derives
from me, from my life and therefore there is love of the other
person and being loved by him because he is a piece of me.
All these things are to Adam the bodily representation of the
limit which is to make the limit easier to bear; which will
enable him to bear it in love. The other person is the limit
placed upon me by God. I love this limit and I shall not
transgress it because of my love. This means nothing except
that the two, who remain *two* as creatures of God, become
one body, i.e. belong to one another in love. In the creation
of the other person freedom and creatureliness are bound
together in love. That is why the other person is grace to the
first, just as the prohibition to eat of the tree of knowledge
was grace. In this common bearing of the limit by the first

two human beings in community is tested the character of this community as the Church. This means that one thing is certain, that where love towards the other is destroyed man can only hate his limit. Then he only wants to possess or deny the other person without limit. For now he is appealing to *his* contribution, to his claim upon the other person, to the origin of the other person in him; what he hitherto received humbly now becomes the occasion for glorification and revolt. That is our world. The grace of the other person, who is our helper because he helps us to bear our limit, i.e. he helps us to live before God, in community with whom we alone can live before God—this grace becomes a curse, the other person becomes the one who makes our hatred of God more passionate than ever. He is now the one on whose account we can no longer live before God. He is our judgment again and again. From this starting point marriage and community are bound to have a new meaning. The power of the other person, in which I live in the presence of God has now become the power of the other person by which I must die before God. The power of life becomes power of destruction, power of community becomes power of isolation, power of love becomes power of hate.

◆ ◆ ◆

Therefore a man leaves his father and his mother and cleaves to his wife, and they become one flesh.

It could be said that here the narrator is obviously stumbling. How can Adam, who knows nothing of a father or a mother, say such a thing? We could also say this is the narrator's practical application of the story, or something of the kind. Really, though, we recognize a basic fact here which has so far been hidden and which has now, as it were unintentionally, come to light. We ourselves are the Adam who speaks. We have a father and a mother and we know the uniqueness of belonging to one another in the love of man and woman, but for us this knowledge has been wholly spoilt and destroyed by our guilt. This passage does not justify running away from the worldly order or from our connexion with our father and mother. It is the profoundest way possible of describing the depth and seriousness of belonging to one another. This ultimate belonging to one another is undoubtedly seen here in connexion with man's sexuality. Very clearly sexuality is the expression of the two-sidedness of being both an individual and being one with the other person. Sexuality is nothing but the ultimate realization of our belonging to one another. Here sexuality has as yet no life of its own detached from this purpose. Here the community of man and woman is the community derived from God, the community of love glorifying and worshipping him as the Creator. It is therefore the Church in its original form. And because it is the Church it is a community eternally bound together. For us such statements do not imply the glorification of our marriages; they are the indication that for us at any rate the connexion between man and woman is not such an unequivocally real one and that the Church's action in the marriage ceremony is perhaps the most questionable of all the Church's official actions. The community of love has been torn to pieces by sexuality and become passion. Therefore it affirms itself and denies the other person as God's creature. This community rests upon the claim that the one makes upon his share in the other—upon his rib in the other, upon the other's having his origin in him. This community is plainly not the glorification of the Creator—in which the Creator once again does the work of his creation upon the unknowing, sleeping Adam and Eve. It is man's snatching for himself the strength and the glory of the Creator—the ascent of man to unconscious awareness of his own ego, to begetting and giving birth out of his own power, in the waking of drunkenness. Of course, this abysmal destruction of the original state does not abolish the fact that, in the truest sense, the community of man and woman is intended to be the Church (Eph. 5.30-32).

◆◆◆

And the man and his wife were both naked, and were not ashamed.

Shame only exists as a result of the knowledge of the division of man, of the division of the world in general, therefore also from knowledge's perception of its own division. Shame is the expression of the fact that we no longer accept the other person as the gift of God. Shame expresses my passionate desire for the other person and the knowledge that belongs to it that the other person is no longer satisfied just to belong to me but desires something from me. Shame covers me before the other because of my own evil and of his evil, because of the division that has come between us. Where the one accepts the other as the companion given to him by God, where he is content with understanding himself as beginning from and ending in the other and in belonging to him, man is not ashamed. In the unity of unbroken obedience man is naked in the presence of man, uncovered, revealing both body and soul, and yet he is not ashamed. Shame only comes into existence in the world of division. Knowledge, death, sexuality—here and in the next chapter we are dealing with the connexion between these three primaeval words of life.

PART 3

I.

THE RELIGIOUS QUESTION

3.1-3 Now the serpent was more subtle than any other wild creature that the Lord God had made. He said to the woman, "Did God say, 'You shall not eat of any tree of the garden'?" And the woman said to the serpent, "We may eat of the fruit of the trees of the garden; but God said, 'You shall not eat of the fruit of the tree which is in the midst of the garden, neither shall you touch it, lest you die.'"

The command not to eat of the tree of knowledge, the creation of Eve, and the serpent must be understood as a connected series in the assault upon the tree of life. They all come from God the Creator and yet, strange to say, they form a common front with man against the Creator. The prohibition which Adam heard as grace becomes law, causing anger in man and in God. Woman, who was created as a companion for man, to help him bear his limit, becomes a seducer. The serpent, one creature of God among others, itself becomes an instrument of evil.

How does this happen? The Bible does not give an answer, at any rate not a direct or an unequivocal one; characteristically it answers indirectly. We would be simplifying and completely distorting the biblical narrative if we were simply to involve the devil, who, as God's enemy, caused all this. This is just what the Bible does not say, for very definite reasons. Similarly, we would misinterpret the context completely if we lay the blame on man's freedom for good and evil, and not on his wrong use of this freedom. It is the characteristic and essential thing about the biblical narrative that the whole event takes place in the world created by God and that no

diaboli ex machina are set in motion to make this inconceivable event understandable and to dramatize it. The double
light in which the creation and evil appear here cannot be
resolved in any way without destroying the central point. The
ambiguity of the serpent, of Eve, and of the tree of knowledge as creatures of the grace of God and as the place of the
voice of evil must be maintained as such and must not be
crudely torn asunder in an unambiguous interpretation. The
twilight, the double light in which the creation appears here
is the only possible form in which man in the middle can
speak of this event, and the Yahwist too was man in the
middle. Only in this way can we, as we must, both put the
guilt completely on to man and at the same time stress that
the guilt is inconceivable, inexplicable and inexcusable. It is
not the purpose of the Bible to give information about the
origin of evil but to witness to its character as guilt and as
the infinite burden of man. To ask about the origin of evil
independently of this is far from the mind of the biblical
writer, and for this very reason the answer cannot be unequivocal and direct. It will always contain two aspects that as a
creature of God I have committed a completely anti-godly
and evil act, and that for that very reason I am guilty—and
moreover inexcusably guilty. It will never be possible simply
to blame the devil who has led us astray. The devil will always
be in the place where I ought to have lived and did not wish
to live as God's creature in God's world. It is of course just as
impossible to blame the creation for being imperfect and
make it responsible for my evil. The guilt rests upon me
alone, I have committed evil in the midst of the primaeval
state of creation. The full inconceivability of this act is expressed here in Gen. 3 by the fact that it is not an evil force
from somewhere or other that suddenly breaks forth into
creation. No, this evil is completely hidden within the world
of creation and occurs in the creation through man. If there
had previously been an account of the Fall of Lucifer, as
Catholic Dogmatics and as Luther too would have it, Adam
would be Lucifer's first victim and as such, he would in principle be relieved his burden. But the unadorned biblical ac-

count says in fact that the Fall was prepared and took place in the midst of creation, and it is just by this means that its complete inexcusability is expressed in the plainest possible way.

◆◆◆

Now the serpent was more subtle than any other wild creature that the Lord God had made.

It is not simply said that the serpent is the devil. The serpent is a creature of God, but it is more subtle than all the others. In the entire story the devil incarnate is never introduced. And yet evil does take place: through man, through the serpent, through the tree. In the first place it is only the Word of God itself which is used once more. The serpent asks, *"Did God say, You shall not eat of any tree in the garden'?"* The serpent does not dispute this word but it enables man to catch sight of a hitherto unknown profundity in which he would be in the position to establish or dispute whether a word is the Word of God or not. The serpent itself in the first place only suggests the possibility that man has perhaps misunderstood here, since God could not possibly have meant it in this way. God, the good Creator, would not impose such a thing upon his creature; this would be a limitation of his love.

The decisive point is that this question suggests to man that he should go behind the Word of God and establish what it is by himself, out of his understanding of the being of God. Should it contradict this understanding then man has clearly made a mistake. Surely it can only serve God's cause if such false words of God, such misunderstood commands are swept aside before it is too late. The misleading thing about this question is therefore that it obviously wants to be thought to come from God. For the sake of the true God it seems to want to sweep aside the given Word of God. Beyond this given Word of God the serpent pretends somehow to know something about the profundity of the true God who is so badly misrepresented in this human word. The serpent claims to know more about God than man, who depends on God's Word alone. The serpent knows of a greater, nobler

God who does not need such a prohibition. In some way it wants to be itself the dark root from which the visible tree of God then springs up. And from this position of power the serpent fights against the Word of God. It knows that it only has power where it claims to come from God, to be pleading his cause. It is evil only as the religious serpent.[1] The serpent, which derives its existence only from the power of God in the question it is asking and which can be evil only where it is religious, now claims to be the power that is behind the Word of God, from which God himself in the first place draws his power.

The serpent's question was a thoroughly religious one. But with the first religious question in the world evil has come upon the scene. Where evil appears in its godlessness it is powerlessness, it is a bogey, we do not need to fear it. In this form it does not concentrate its power but diverts us from the other place where it really desires to break through. And here it is wrapped in the garment of religiousness. The wolf in sheep's clothing, Satan in an angel's form of light: this is the shape appropriate to evil. "Did God say?", that plainly is the godless question. "Did God say," that he is love, that he wishes to forgive our sins, that we need only believe him, that we need no works, that Christ has died and been raised for us, that we shall have eternal life in his kingdom, that we are no longer alone but upheld by God's grace, that one day all sorrow and wailing shall have an end? "Did God say," thou shalt not steal, thou shalt not commit adultery, thou shalt not bear false witness . . . did he really say it to me? Perhaps it does not apply in my particular case? "Did God say," that he is a God who is wrathful towards those who do not keep his commandments? Did he demand the sacrifice of Christ? I know better that he is the infinitely good, the all-loving father.

This is the question that appears innocuous but through it evil wins power in us, through it we become disobedient to God. If we met this question in its real godlessness we should

[1] The German reads "die fromme Schlange"; "fromme" means both "pious" and "religious." [Tr.]

be able to resist it. But that is not the way to attack Christians. They must be approached with God himself, they must be shown a better, prouder God than they seem to have, if they are to fall. What is the real evil in this question? It is not that it is asked at all. It is that the false answer is contained within it, that within it is attacked the basic attitude of the creature towards the Creator. Man is expected to be judge of God's word instead of simply hearing and doing it. This is accomplished as follows. On the basis of an idea, a principle, some previously gained knowledge about God, man is now to judge God's concrete Word. When man proceeds against the concrete Word of God with the weapon of a principle, with an idea of God, he is in the right from the first, he becomes God's master, he has left the path of obedience, he has withdrawn from God's addressing him. In other words, in this question the possibility is played off against the reality and the possibility undermines the reality. However, in man's relationship to God there are no possibilities, there is only reality. There is no ". . . allow me . . . ," there is only command and obedience.

For the first man, who lives entirely within this reality, this appeal to what is possible for him—i.e. not to obey the Word of God—is equivalent to being addressed in his freedom in which he entirely belongs to God; it is only made possible when this possibility of disobedience towards God is wrapped up in the reality of his "being for God." Only because the question is asked in a way that Adam can understand it as a new possibility of "being for God" can it lead him to "being against God." The possibility of our *own* "will to be for God," discovered by ourselves, is the real evil in the serpent's question. It is not a piece of stupidity, it is the very summit of the serpent's cunning that it exaggerates so grossly in this question, *"Did God say, You shall not eat of any tree in the garden?"* With this it has Eve on its side from the very first, indeed, it compels her to the confession, No naturally God did not say that. The fact that Eve must qualify something regarding a Word of God—even if it is falsely represented— must throw her into the greatest confusion. It must indeed enable her to feel, for the first time, the attraction of making judgments about the Word of God. By means of the obviously false the serpent will now bring down that which is right.

Let us be on our guard against such cunning exaggerations of God's command. The evil one is certainly in them. The serpent's question immediately proved to be *the* satanic question *par excellence, the* question that robs God of his honour and aims to divert man from the Word of God. While appearing to be religious this question attacks God as the ultimate presupposition of all existence. Man cannot resist it except by saying ὕπαγε, Σατανᾶ.[1] Eve's answer still remains on the plane of ignorance. She does not know or recognize evil and she can therefore do nothing but repeat the given commandment and put it correctly. That is a great deal; she remains true to the commandment. However, she does become involved in this clever conversation; it has struck some spark in her. But the old order is still intact. Man cannot go behind God's Word. The tree of knowledge and the tree of life remain untouched.

---

[1] "Begone, Satan" (Matt. 4.10).

II.

SICUT DEUS

3.4-5 But the serpent said to the woman, "You will not die. For God knows that when you eat of it your eyes will be opened, and you will be like God, knowing good and evil."

The first passage of conversation is over. But Eve's answer does not exclude a new onset by the serpent. Thus the conversation goes on—the first conversation about God, the first religious, theological conversation. It is not prayer or calling upon God together but speaking about God, going beyond him. Inasmuch as Eve has involved herself in this conversation the serpent can now risk the real attack. It speaks about God, and indeed with an attitude of deep knowledge of the secrets of God, i.e. it speaks religiously. But this religiousness is now unmasked in open attack. "*Did* God say?" "Yes he *did* say . . . but why did he say it?" That is how the conversation continues. "He has said it out of envy. . . . God is not good but evil, tormenting . . . be intelligent, be more intelligent than your God and take what he grudges you. . . . He has said it, indeed you are right, Eve, but he has lied. God's Word is lie . . . because you will not die."

That the lie portrays the truth as lie is the ultimate possible rebellion. It is the abyss of the lie that it lives because it sets itself up as truth and condemns the truth as lie.

◆ ◆ ◆

"You will not die. For God knows that when you eat of it your eyes will be opened and you will be like God, knowing good and evil."

The Creator himself has said that this tree would mediate knowledge; the only difference is that whereas the Creator had decreed death for this deed, the serpent connects it to the promise of being like God. To anticipate something we must say later, man's becoming like God, promised by the serpent, can be nothing but what the Creator calls death. It is true that man becomes *sicut deus* through the Fall but this very man *sicut deus* can live no longer; he is dead. That means that the serpent, in all its attempts to portray the truth of God as lie can never escape this truth. On the contrary, in its lie the serpent must even agree with it, because it is speaking of the death of man, but in another form. We shall return to this later.

Here we stand at the last point to which the biblical author takes man before the abyss comes and the inconceivable, infinite chasm opens. The series of events—from God's prohibition and the creation of woman to the serpent's question —which we find in battle together against the tree of life, here reaches its end. In what does this final approach to the inconceivable consist? Let us repeat here, that the point in question cannot be an approach to the conceivable but exclusively an approach to the inconceivable. By this approach the inconceivable is intended to be left in its complete inconceivability and unpardonableness.

"You will not die." "You shall die." In these two statements the world gapes asunder for Adam. Statement stands against statement. This is beyond his power of comprehension, for how is he to know what a lie is? Truth against truth—God's truth against serpent's truth, God's truth connected with the prohibition, the serpent's truth connected with the promise, God's truth pointing to my limit, the serpent's truth pointing to my limitlessness both are truth, both come from God, God against God. And this second God is at the same time the God of the promise to man to be like God. God against man-like-God. God and *imago dei* man against God and *sicut*

deus man. *Imago dei*—Godlike man in his existence for God
and neighbour, in his primitive creatureliness and limitation;
sicut deus—Godlike man in his out-of-himself knowledge of
good and evil, in his limitlessness and his acting out-of-
himself, in his underived existence, in his loneliness. *Imago
dei*—that is, man bound to the Word of the Creator and
living from him; *sicut deus*—that is, man bound to the depths
of his own knowledge about God, in good and evil; *imago dei*
—the creature living in the unity of obedience; *sicut deus*—
the creator-man living out of the division of good and evil.
Imago dei, sicut deus, agnus dei—the One who was sacrificed
for man *sicut deus*, killing man's false divinity in true divinity,
the God-Man who restores the image of God.

How can Adam understand the serpent's promise that he
shall be like God? At any rate, not as the devilish promise of
death and revolt against the Creator. He does not in any way
know of the possibility of evil, and cannot understand it except as the possibility of being more devout, of being more
obedient than he is in his *imago dei* structure. For Adam
sicut deus can only be a new possibility within the given
possibility of the *imago dei* creature. It can only signify a new,
a deeper kind of creaturely being. He is bound to understand
the serpent in this way. Certainly he sees that the new, deeper
kind of creaturely being must be purchased through the
transgression of the commandment. And this fact must make
him attentive. He is really between God and God, or, better,
between God and the idol, and the idol portrays itself as the
true God. But what is the idol for Adam except the very
impossibility of being a creature? What can the idol do but
show Adam anew his dependence upon the Creator? What
can this promise of being like God be except a deeper kind
of being for God or allowing him a firmer grasp on the given
reality of the Creator and his Word? What can the idol be for
him but the final, the deepest indication of the only true
Word of God, of God the Creator? What is the idol to Adam
other than the ultimate grace in which God binds himself to
man? What is Eve's religious conversation with the serpent
other than the final sealing of the exclusive right of the Cre-

ator over man? Therefore how can Eve's answer be anything but praise for the incomparable, inconceivable grace of the Creator, which now breaks forth from the *ultimate* depth of her creatureliness and freedom for God and her neighbour?

THE FALL

3.6 So when the woman saw that the tree was good for food, and that it was a delight to the eyes, and that the tree was to be desired to make one wise, she took of its fruit and ate; and she also gave some to her husband, and he ate.

Instead of some answer, instead of any further theological discussion with the serpent, there is the act. We ask what has happened. In the first place the middle has been entered, the limit has been transgressed. Now man stands in the middle, now he is without limit. That he stands in the middle means that now he lives out of his own resources and no longer from the middle. That he is without a limit means that he is alone. To be in the middle and to be alone means to be like God. Man is *sicut deus*. Now he lives out of himself, now he creates his own life, he is his own creator. He no longer needs the Creator, he has become a creator himself, to the extent that he creates his own life. With this his creatureliness is finished and destroyed for him. Adam is no longer creature. He has torn himself away from his creatureliness. He *is* like God, and this "is" is meant very seriously. It is not that he feels himself so, but that he *is*. Together with *the limit* Adam has lost *his creatureliness*. Limitless Adam can no longer be addressed in his creatureliness.

This brings us to a central point. Creatureliness and the Fall are not related to one another in such a way that the Fall is an act of creatureliness, which cannot abolish creatureliness, which at most has the power to modify or damage it. On the contrary, the Fall *really* makes a creator, the *sicut deus* man, out of the creature, the *imago dei* man. Above all, there is for the time being no more right to address the *sicut deus* man in his creatureliness. There is no possibility of recognizing him in his creatureliness, just because he really is like God. From this point on no one can make any statement about man without bearing in mind the fact—or losing sight of the fact—that he is like God. The reason is that such a statement would have to come from beyond man but that the limitless man admits nothing beyond from which anything can be said about him. Man's being *sicut deus* in fact includes his not wanting to be a creature. Only God himself could address man in a different way. He can address man in his never-abolished creatureliness, and he does this in Jesus Christ, in the Cross and in the Church. He speaks of the creatureliness of man only as the truth which is spoken by God and which, because of God, we believe in spite of all our knowledge of reality.

Wherein does man's being like God consist? It is in his attempt to want to be "for God" himself, to ordain a new way of "being for God," in a special way of being religious. And this religiousness consists in man's going behind the given Word of God and procuring his own knowledge of God. This possibility of knowing about God beyond his given Word is man's being like God; for whence is man to take this knowledge if not from the springs of his own life and being? This means that for his knowledge of God man renounces the Word of God which constantly descends upon him out of the unenterable middle and limit of life. Man renounces life from this Word and snatches it for himself. He is himself in the middle. Therefore man's being like God is disobedience in the form of obedience, it is will to power in the form of service, it is desire to be a creator in the form of creatureliness, it is being dead in the form of life.

How has this come about? We shall answer this question biblically as follows: first, we shall demonstrate again the series of events that—after the event—must be understood

as leading up to it. Secondly we shall point to the infinite
chasm lying between the end of this series and the act itself.
Thirdly we shall ask the question as such correctly by taking
the theological question out of the speculative one and an-
swering it.

I. In principle it is never wrong to picture to oneself the
series of events preceding an evil deed. Everything however
depends upon never making the series of events responsible
for the deed as such; the series must go no further than
the point where the chasm opens, where it becomes really
inconceivable how the evil could have been committed. Reference back to the series of events preceding the deed may
only be made use of for this purpose. At the beginning of the
series there is the prohibition laid upon Adam. It indicated
to Adam his creatureliness and his freedom, which can only
be understood as freedom for God. Thus this prohibition
must have made the grace of the Creator only more visible
to Adam. But this very being addressed in his creatureliness
and freedom made the distance between the Creator and the
creature more distinct, and thus at the same time it must
have emphasized the creature's own being. In the creation of
woman from Adam's rib, Adam's own being as creature is
intensified in a way he had never imagined. The limit within
which he lives has now taken on bodily form. Of course he
loves this form of the other person but he also knows that in
her is a piece of himself, so that she makes him attentive to
his rights and therefore again to his own personal being.
Man's limit has drawn nearer to him and has become all the
more sharply defined. But it is just this bodily revelation of
the limit in the love for the other person which gives Adam
an ever deeper knowledge of the grace of the Creator. With
the creation of woman, man's limit has entered into the midst
of the created world. But with this event the danger of the
transgression of the limit was not greater but, on the contrary,
smaller, for Adam must now worship God the more fervently
as his only Creator. It is clear, however, that, for the Fall, if
the limit were to be transgressed in opposition to the Creator
this would have to coincide with the transgression of the limit

within the world of creation. Every transgression of the limit is bound to mean at the same time an attack upon the creatureliness of the other person. The violation of the tree of knowledge has to be at the same time a violation of the other person. But is it possible to speak of danger where the unbroken unity of obedience must make impossible every thought of the transgression of the given limit, where the limit is known only as grace?

The final point is that man was made attentive to the fact that his obedience and the object of his obedience were two very different things, that he did not necessarily have to allow his obedience to be determined by its object; that his obedience to God did not necessarily have to consist in not eating of the fruit. This means that now his freedom in unbroken obedience *as distinct from* his creatureliness has brought him to a particular consciousness, i.e. that his freedom is set over against his creatureliness as a second, a different thing. And yet his way of being aware of this is only that his freedom is a part of his creatureliness; that is, that it is only to be used in service, in service to God. Here man knows with ultimate clarity about himself in the presence of God. And again we ask, why is there no outbreak here in the world of creation, of rejoicing, of thanks and praise of the Creator, never ending and never willing to end? Why is this not new strength for new obedience?

Eve falls first. She falls as the weaker one, as the one partly taken from the man. But there is no excuse for her fall, she is completely herself. Yet the culmination of the story is the fall of Adam. Eve only falls totally when Adam falls, for the two are one. Adam falls because of Eve, Eve falls because of Adam, the two are one. In their guilt too they are two and yet one. They fall together as one and each one carries all the guilt alone. Male and female he created them—and man fell away from him—male and female.

How could it happen that Eve's act did not ultimately turn Adam's attention towards his Creator? He could not comprehend what Eve had done. He could grasp this too only as an infinite strengthening of the word of the serpent, which pointed towards his creatureliness and freedom for God. *And he ate.*

II. There are three things to understand. First, the inconceivability of the act and hence its lack of excuse. The reason for this event cannot be uncovered either in the nature of man, or in that of the creation, or in the nature of the serpent. No theory of *posse peccare* or of *non posse peccare* can apprehend the fact that the deed was actually done. Every attempt to make it understandable is merely the accusation which the creature hurls against the Creator. Secondly, this act, from man's point of view, is conclusive. Man cannot go back upon it. Otherwise Adam could absolve himself from his guilt. His guilt would not be guilt and Christ would have died in vain. Thirdly, this act of man whom God created as man and woman is a deed of mankind from which no man can absolve himself. The guilt of the act becomes boundless because no man commits it for himself but each man is guilty of the deed of the other. Adam falls because of Eve, Eve because of Adam. Not in such a way, however, that the other person immediately takes my burden away but so that he burdens me infinitely with his guilt.

The Fall of man in God's creation is both inconceivable and unalterably inexcusable, and therefore the word "disobedience" does not exhaust the facts of the case. It is revolt, it is the creature's departure from the attitude which is the only possible attitude for him, it is the creature's becoming Creator, it is the destruction of creatureliness. It is defection, it is the fall from being held in creatureliness. This defection is a continual falling, a plunging into bottomless depths, a being relinquished, a withdrawal ever farther and deeper. And in all this it is not simply a moral lapse but the destruction of creation by the creature. The Fall affects the whole of the created world which is henceforth plundered of its creatureliness as it crashes blindly into infinite space, like a meteor which has torn away from its nucleus. It is of this fallen-falling world that we must now speak.

III. The question of why evil exists is not a theological question, for it assumes that it is possible to go behind the existence forced upon us as sinners. If we could answer it then *we* would not be sinners. We could make something else responsible. Therefore the "question of why" can always only be answered with the "that," which burdens man completely.

The theological question does not arise about the origin of evil but about the real overcoming of evil on the Cross; it asks for the forgiveness of guilt, for the reconciliation of the fallen world.

IV

THE NEW

3.7 Then the eyes of both were opened, and they knew that they were naked; and they sewed fig leaves together and made themselves aprons.

"The end of the ways of God is bodiliness." It does not say "they knew and recognized good and evil," but *the eyes of both were opened, and they saw that they were naked.* Can we really understand the whole story from here by saying that the point at issue is the origin of the love of man and woman? Can we say that eating of the tree of knowledge has been the great, proud, liberating act of man by means of which he has won the right of love and of creating life? Was the knowledge of good and evil essentially the new knowledge of a boy become man? In the last resort, was Adam's only mistake not to storm straight away from the tree of knowledge to the tree of life in order to eat also of its fruit? The correct part of all this is that the point at issue here is the problem of sexuality. For Adam, who lives in unity, the knowledge of good and evil is the impossible knowledge of the duality and the rupture of the whole. The comprehensive expression of this duality is *tob* and *ra,* in our language full of pleasure and therefore good, full of pain and therefore evil. And it is just this combination of pleasureful and good that takes all the weight from the moralistic interpretation. In the divided, fallen world the pleasureful is ultimately as serious as the "good," since both have equally fallen from the primaeval unity. Both exist only in duality and do not find the way back to unity.

This division in *tob* and *ra* must first of all express itself in Adam's relation to Eve. Eve, the other person, had been to Adam the bodily form of the given limit whom he acknowledged in love, i.e. in the undivided unity of his devotion and whom he loved in her very nature as limit, i.e. *because* she was human and yet "another person." Now that he has transgressed the limit, he knows for the first time that he was limited. At the same time he no longer accepts the limit as the grace of God the Creator but hates it, looking upon it as the envy of God the Creator. In the same act he has transgressed the limit that the other person had embodied for him. Now he no longer sees the limit of the other person as grace but as the wrath, the hatred, the envy of God. This means that he no longer sees the other person in love. He sees him over against himself, at variance with himself. Now the limit is no longer grace, holding man in the unity of his creaturely and free love; it is discord. Man and woman are divided. This means two things. First of all, man makes use of his share in the woman's body; more generally, one man makes use of his right to the other and puts forward his claim to the possession of the other, thereby denying and destroying the other person's creatureliness.

This avid passion of man for the other person first comes to expression in sexuality. The sexuality of the man who has transgressed his limit is the refusal to recognize any limit whatever; it is the boundless passion to be without a limit. Sexuality is the passionate hatred of every limit, it is arbitrariness to the highest degree, it is self-will, it is avid, impotent will for unity in the divided world. It is avid because it knows of man's common humanity from the origin onwards, and impotent because together with his limit man has finally lost the other person. Sexuality desires the destruction of the other person as creature; it robs him of his creatureliness, violates him as well as his limit, hates grace. Man's own life is to preserve and propagate itself in this destruction of the other person. Man is creative in destroying. In sexuality mankind preserves itself in its destruction. Unrestrained sexuality, like uncreative sexuality, is therefore destruction *par excellence*. Thus it is an insane acceleration of the Fall; it is self-affirmation to the point of self-destruction. Passion and hate, *tob* and *ra*—these are the fruit of the tree of knowledge.

Now from this division it follows secondly that man covers himself. Man without a limit, hating, avidly passionate, does not show himself in his nakedness. Nakedness is the essence of unity and of unbrokenness, of being for the other, of objectivity, of the recognition of the other in his right, in his limiting me and in his creatureliness. Nakedness is the essence of the ignorance of the possibility of robbing the other of this right. Nakedness is revelation, nakedness believes in grace. Nakedness does not know it is naked, as the eye does not see or know itself. Nakedness is innocence. To cover is the essence of a world split into *tob* and *ra,* therefore in the world of *tob* and *ra* revelation must veil itself. But the greatest contradiction here is that man, who has come to be without a limit, is bound to point to his limit without intending to do so. He covers himself because he feels shame. In shame man acknowledges his limit. It is the peculiar dialectic of the torn world that man lives in it without a limit, therefore as the One. Yet he always lives hating the limit and he therefore lives as one divided. The dialectic is that he is ashamed as one naked. Man's shame is his reluctant acknowledgment of revelation, of the limit, of the other person, of God. Therefore the preservation of shame in the fallen world is the only —although a most contradictory—possibility of acknowledging the original nakedness and the blessedness of this nakedness. This is not because shame is something good in itself— that is the moralistic, puritanical totally unbiblical interpretation—but because it must give reluctant witness to its own fallen state.

If the dogmatics of the Church saw the essence of original sin in sexuality, this is not such nonsense as Protestants have often said from a point of view of moralistic naturalism. The knowledge of *tob* and *ra* is originally not an abstract knowledge of ethical principles, but sexuality; i.e. a perversion of the relationship between persons. And since the essential nature of sexuality consists in destruction, the dark secret of the originally sinful being of man is in fact preserved from generation to generation in continuing procreation. The objection, which refers to the natural character of sexuality, is not conscious of the highly ambivalent character of all so-called "natural" things in our world. The sanctification of sexuality is given in its restraint by shame, i.e. in its covering and in the vocation of the restrained community of marriage in the Church. The deepest reason for this is that man has lost his creatureliness. His creatureliness has been corrupted in his being like God. All the world of creation is now veiled: it is mute and unresponsive, opaque and mysterious. The world of *sicut deus* man is ashamed before him, it hides from his view.

V

FLIGHT

3.8-13 And they heard the sound of the Lord God
walking in the garden in the cool of the day, and the man
and his wife hid themselves from the presence of the Lord
God among the trees of the garden. But the Lord God
called to the man, and said to him, "Where are you?"
And he said, "I heard the sound of thee in the garden,
and I was afraid, because I was naked; and I hid myself."
He said, "Who told you that you were naked? Have you
eaten of the tree which I commanded you not to eat?"
The man said, "The woman whom thou gavest to be with
me, she gave me fruit of the tree, and I ate." Then the
Lord God said to the woman, "What is this that you have
done?" The woman said, "The serpent beguiled me, and I
ate."

Adam, knowing *tob* and *ra,* having fallen from unity into division, can no longer stand before his Creator. He has transgressed the limit and now he hates his limit, he denies it, he is like God, without a limit. But just as in shame he reluctantly acknowledges the limit of the other person, so he unwillingly agrees with God his Creator by fleeing from him, by hiding from him. He does not insolently confront God but when he hears God's voice he hides from him. What a strange delusion of Adam's, both then and today, to think that he can hide from God, as though the world were opaque to God where it appears covered, veiled and opaque to us after we have fallen with it. Man has suddenly fallen from God and is still in flight. The Fall is not enough for him; he cannot flee fast enough.

This flight, Adam's hiding from God, we call conscience. Before the Fall there was no conscience. Man has only been divided in himself since his division from the Creator. And indeed it is the function of the conscience to put man to flight from God. Thus, unwillingly, it agrees with God, and on the other hand in this flight it allows man to feel secure in his hiding place. This means that it deludes man into feeling that he really is fleeing. Moreover it allows him to believe that this flight is his triumphal procession and all the world is fleeing from him. Conscience drives man from God into a secure hiding place. Here, distant from God, man plays the judge himself and just by this means he escapes God's judgment. Now man really lives by his own good and evil, from the innermost division within himself. Conscience is shame before God in which at the same time our own wickedness is concealed, in which man justifies himself and in which, on the other hand, the acknowledgment of the other person is reluctantly preserved. Conscience is not the voice of God to sinful man; it is man's defence against it, but as this defence it points towards it, contrary to our will and knowledge.

"Adam, where are you?" With this word the Creator calls Adam forth out of his conscience, Adam must stand before his Creator. Man is not allowed to remain in his sin alone, God speaks to him, he stops him in his flight. "Come out of your hiding-place, from your self-reproach, your covering, your secrecy, your self-torment, from your vain remorse . . . confess to yourself, do not lose yourself in religious despair, be yourself, Adam . . . where are you? Stand before your Creator." This call goes directly against the conscience, for the conscience says: "Adam, you are naked, hide yourself from the Creator, you dare not stand before him." God says: "Adam, stand before me." God kills the conscience. The fleeing Adam must realize that he cannot flee from his Creator.

We have all had the dream that we desire to flee from something horrible and cannot. This is the ever-recurring knowledge in our subconscious of this true situation of fallen man. The same thing is now expressed in Adam's answer: *I was naked and I hid myself.* Adam tries to excuse himself with something that accuses him, he attempts to flee further and yet he knows he has already been apprehended. "I am

sinful, I cannot stand before thee," as though sin were an
excuse. Inconceivable folly of man: "just because you are a
sinner, stand before me and do not flee."

But still Adam holds his ground. *The woman whom thou
gavest to be with me, she gave me of the fruit of the tree, and
I ate.* He confesses his sin, but as he confesses, he takes to
flight again. "You have given me the woman, not I, I am not
guilty, you are guilty." The double light of creation and sin is
exploited. "The woman is surely your creature, it is your own
work that has caused me to fall. Why have you brought forth
an imperfect creation, and is it my fault?" So instead of sur-
rendering Adam falls back on one art learned from the serpent, that of correcting the idea of God, of appealing from
God the Creator to a better, a different God. That is, he flees
again. The woman takes to flight with him and blames the
serpent; that is, she really blames the Creator of the serpent.
Adam has not surrendered, he has not confessed. He has
appealed to his conscience, to his knowledge of good and
evil, and out of this knowledge he has accused his Creator.
He has not recognized the grace of the Creator which proves
itself true by the fact that he calls Adam, by the fact that he
does not let him flee. Adam sees this grace only as hate, as
wrath, and this wrath kindles his own hate, his rebellion, his
will to escape from God. Adam remains in the Fall. The Fall
accelerates and becomes infinite.

VI.

CURSE AND PROMISE

3.14-19 The Lord God said to the serpent, "Because you have done this, cursed are you above all cattle, and above all wild animals; upon your belly you shall go, and dust you shall eat all the days of your life. I will put enmity between you and the woman, and between your seed and her seed; he shall bruise your head, and you shall bruise his heel." To the woman he said, "I will greatly multiply your pain in childbearing; in pain you shall bring forth children, yet your desire shall be for your husband, and he shall rule over you." And to Adam he said, "Because you have listened to the voice of your wife, and have eaten of the tree of which I commanded you, 'You shall not eat of it,' cursed is the ground because of you; in toil you shall eat of it all the days of your life; thorns and thistles it shall bring forth to you; and you shall eat the plants of the field. In the sweat of your face you shall eat bread till you return to the ground, for out of it you were taken; you are dust, and to dust you shall return."

We are approaching the end. With curse and promise God speaks to the fallen, unreconciled, fleeing Adam. Adam is preserved alive in a world between curse and promise, and the last promise is the permission to die. Paradise is destroyed.

"*Woe, woe, you have destroyed the beautiful world with a mighty hand. It falls, it decays. Mighty one of the sons of earth, rebuild it more splendidly, erect it again within your breast!*"[1] This is just what does not apply here. On the contrary, here the meaning is, "Now live in this destroyed world, you cannot escape it, live in it between curse and promise." The curse and the promise are laid upon the fallen Adam in

[1] From *Faust*, I. [Tr.]

four great thoughts: enmity with the serpent, the pain of childbirth, the burden of labour, and death. Curse and promise are extended to the same thing. The curse is the affirmation of the fallen world by the Creator: man *must* live in the fallen world; man has his way, he must live like God in his *sicut deus* world. That is the curse. He *may* live in it. He is not without the Word of God, even though it is the wrathful, repelling, cursing Word of God. This is the promise. Thus Adam lives between curse and promise.

Curse and promise consist in the first place of the eternal enmity in which man is placed towards the serpent, towards the power of religious godlessness. In the destroyed world between God's curse and his promise man is tempted. He does not receive the Word of God in peace and tranquillity, he becomes aware of it when the religious question is asked in the wrong way. Man does not adhere to God in peace but in enmity and conflict. But in this curse-laden destiny he is given the promise of victory that is ever newly won, in which man bruises the serpent's head. Of course, man also remains behind wounded in this battle. The conquered serpent still bruises man's heel. The battle for the Word of God marks him with scars. Man is not to be a hero, he shall be locked in battle, ever newly victorious and ever newly wounded, and all his kind with him. In this battle, which he takes upon himself as curse and as promise and through which he fights, man is allowed to live. The new things that the tree of knowledge brought upon Adam and Eve were shame and passion.

The visible sign of this division of the primaeval unity, of the innermost rupture of the intercourse of man and woman, is the pain that woman bears as the fruit of passionate intercourse with man. Pain is inseparably united with the new thing, with the pleasure of passion. *Tob* and *ra*, the pleasureful and the painful enter into human life united as brothers. The knowledge of pain increases pleasure and the knowledge of pleasure increases pain. It is woman's humiliation that she must give birth with pain: that she must have desire for the man and yet serve him with pain. She has had her way, she may belong to Adam in her being *sicut deus*, but it is this very thing which is now at once curse and promise. Man must thoroughly taste his new *sicut deus* knowledge of *tob* and *ra*. Thus he may live, he lives before God in the destroyed world, between the curse and the promise of God.

In man's enmity towards the serpent man's relation with God comes under the law of *tob* and *ra*, the law of curse and promise—it is divided. Curse and promise, good and evil in the *community* of man and woman are spoken of in the destiny of woman. Thirdly, God's Word to Adam proclaims the destruction and division of the primal relation between man and *nature*. The ground, for the fruits of which Adam had previously only had to stretch out a hand, which had brought him what he needed, becomes cursed because of Adam's deed. It becomes Adam's concern, his pain, his toil, his enemy. All the other creatures rise up against *sicut deus* man, the creature that tires to live out of his own self. They fail him, they withdraw from him. They grow mute, mysterious and unfruitful. But since they are subject to man they fall with the Fall of man. Nature is without a lord and therefore it is itself rebellious and desperate. It is nature under the curse, the cursed ground. This is our earth, cursed out of the glory of its creation, cast out of the unequivocal directness of its language and of its praise of the Creator into the ambiguity of the absolutely strange and mysterious. The trees, the animals, which had once represented the Word of God the Creator directly, now indicate in often grotesque ways the inconceivability, the arbitrariness of a despot hidden in darkness. Thus the *work* of man upon the cursed ground becomes the expression of the disunion of fallen man with nature; it is under the curse. And at the same time it becomes the expression of a passionate nostalgia for primaeval unity; it is promised that by work man may live together with nature from which he is taken and to which he belongs as a brother. Thus the fruits of the field become both the bread which we eat with tears and the bread of charity, of him who sustains us, who allows man still to live upon the cursed ground, the man who remains true to his mother, the earth, even though she

stands under God's curse. In work man lives between curse
and promise, between *tob* and *ra*, pleasure and pain, but he
lives before God the Creator.

This is the changed, the destroyed, world. At odds with
God, with the other person and with nature, man cannot live,
yet in this division of *tob* and *ra*, he cannot live *without God*,
without the other person, or without nature. In truth he lives
in the world of the curse, but just because it is *God's* curse
that burdens it, this world is not totally forsaken by God; it is
the world of the preservation of life, blessed in God's curse,
pacified in enmity, pain and work.

Preservation for what? To what end? 3.19 says it unmistak-
ably: "*In the sweat of your face you shall eat bread till you
return to the ground, for out of it you were taken; you are
dust, and to dust you shall return.*" The fallen Adam lives on
the way to his death. His life is preserved life on the way to
his death. Why? Because Adam as man *sicut deus* has taken
into himself death with the fruit of the tree of knowledge.
Adam is dead before he dies. The serpent was right: you will
be like God, you will not die; i.e. the death of non-being. But
the Creator was right, too, "*for in the day that you eat of it
you shall die*"; i.e. the death of being like God. Let us now
look at this unheard-of ambiguity: the serpent, with its lie by
which it brings man down, must tell God's truth. Man *sicut
deus* is dead, for he has cut himself off from the tree of life,
he lives out of his own self and yet he cannot live. He must
live and cannot live. That means he is dead.

Now the enmity towards the serpent, the painful community of man and woman and the cursed ground become divine mercy. God has mercy on their ability to live in division.
Man can only live as the one who is preserved in division,
and he can live only on the way to death. He cannot escape
life. Death, this having to return to dust, which burdens man
as the ultimate, the most terrible curse, is now to man who
lives in merciful preservation, a promise of the God of grace.
Adam must understand this death of turning into dust as the
death of his present state of death, of his *sicut deus* being.
The death of death—that is the promise in this curse. Adam

understands it to be sinking back into the nothingness out of which God created the world. To him, the last promise is nothingness: nothingness as the death of death. Therefore to Adam his life is preserved for nothingness. How should Adam, who has fallen from faith, know that death's real death is never nothingness, but is only the living God, that there is indeed no such thing as nothingness, that the promise of the death of death is never nothingness, but only means life, Christ himself? How should Adam know that in this promise of death there was already proclaimed the end of death, the resurrection of the dead? How could Adam hear that in the peace of death, and of the return to mother earth, there is already announced the peace which God would one day conclude with the earth, the peace which he would set up over a newly blessed earth of the world of the resurrection?

VII.

THE MOTHER OF ALL LIVING

3.20 The man called his wife's name Eve, because she was the mother of all living.

Adam shows wild exultation, defiance, insolence, and victory when he gives his wife, over whom this curse has been proclaimed, the name of "mother of all living." It is as if—like Prometheus—he is boasting about robbery that he has committed against his Creator—as though he were defiantly severing himself from the Creator with his booty, his wife, to whom he is bound in a new way by the decree of the curse which will burden both of them from this point on. The fallen Eve is the ancient mother of man from whom all pleasure and pain have taken their beginning; she is the first of the knowing, and all her children, the knowing, those who are tormented by pleasure and pain, look back upon her with thanks and reproaches. For Adam she is the symbol of the new, of the life lived in passion, torn from the Creator. The strange thing is that in Adam's words there are undertones which almost sound like deep thanks which he offers to the Creator for his curse. Strange contradiction: thanks to the Creator that man is preserved in the world estranged from God, thanks to the Creator that man may be like God, thanks to the Creator, because man *sicut deus* does not escape his

Creator in defiance and insolence. Eve, the fallen, wise mother of man—this is the first beginning. Mary, the innocent, unknowing mother of God—this is the second beginning.

VIII.

GOD'S NEW ACTION

*3.21 And the Lord God made for Adam and for his wife
garments of skins, and clothed them.*

The Creator is now the Preserver. The created world is now
the fallen, preserved world. In the world between curse and
promise, between *tob* and *ra,* good and evil, God deals with
man in his own way. *He made them garments,* says the Bible.
That means that God accepts men as they are, as fallen. He
affirms them as fallen. He does not expose them before one
another in their nakedness, he himself covers them. God's
action is concerned with man, but the deciding point is that
it now orders and restrains. God's action does not break
through the new laws of earth and man, it enters into them,
and because it enters into them it is at the same time their
restraint and order. That is, it refers to their evil, their fallen
state. By making garments for men God shows them that
this is necessary because of their wickedness. In this way he
restrains their passion but does not destroy it. God preserves
the world by affirming the sinful world and directing it into
its limits by means of ordinances.[1] But none of these ordinances any longer have any eternal character because they
are only there to preserve life. And we have already said that

[1] The German word is "Ordnung"="order." [Tr.]

for Adam the preservation of life is directed towards death. For us it is directed only towards—Christ. All the orders of our fallen world are God's orders of preservation on the way to Christ. They are not orders of creation but of preservation. They have no value in themselves. They are accomplished and have purpose only through Christ. God's new action towards man is that he preserves him in his fallen world, in his fallen orders, on the way to death, approaching the resurrection, the new creation, on the way to Christ. Man remains between *tob* and *ra,* divided. Further, with his *tob*-good he remains beyond the good of God. With his whole existence split into *tob* and *ra,* in estrangement from God, in the Fall, he remains in the fallen and falling world. He is, therefore, in a twilight. And because he is in a twilight, all his thinking about Creation and Fall is bound to it—the thinking of the biblical author as well—as far as it remains objective thinking and does not become fantastic. Therefore man speaks of paradise and of Adam's fall in the way the Bible speaks of it. He cannot return from division to unity, he is no longer able to distinguish clearly the light of Lucifer, the light-bearer, from the light of God. He remains in the twilight, and God affirms him in this, his new *sicut deus* world, by preserving him there.

IX

THE TREE OF LIFE

3.22ff. Then the Lord God said, "Behold, the man has become like one of us, knowing good and evil; and now, lest he put forth his hand and take also of the tree of life, and eat, and live for ever" — therefore the Lord God sent him forth from the garden of Eden to till the ground from which he was taken. He drove out the man; and at the east of the garden of Eden he placed the cherubim, and a flaming sword which turned every way, to guard the way to the tree of life.

The whole story finally comes to a climax in these verses. The significance of the tree of life, of which so remarkably little had been said earlier, is only really comprehensible here. Indeed, it is now obvious that the whole story has really been about this tree. It could not occur to Adam, who derived his life from God, who lived from this middle, to taste of this tree. The tree of life can only be endangered by the tree of knowledge.

In what way is this true? It is true inasmuch as the fruit of the tree of knowledge, knowing good and evil, was the death of man, inasmuch as man *sicut deus* is not man living but dead. It is true inasmuch as Adam only reaches out for the fruit of the tree of life after he has fallen a prey to death, in order that he need not die in his being *sicut deus* after all. Here there can be no more doubt that the serpent was right in its promise. The Creator confirms it: *the man has become like one of us*. He is *sicut deus*. He has his way. He is himself a creator, a source of life and of the knowledge of good and evil. He is alone, he lives out of his own self, he no longer needs any other person. He is the lord of this world, but now of course the solitary lord and despot of the mute, violated, silenced, dead, world of his ego.

But as man *sicut deus* he cannot really live without enmity towards the serpent—i.e. without God, without the other person or without the other creatures. In conscience and remorse he always seeks to feign the presence, the reality of another in his life; man accuses, torments and glorifies himself only in order to escape by lying from the dreadful loneliness of an echo-less solitude. He knows what he has lost by being *sicut deus*. He knows of his lost life. He knows that he must die. But man is not like God for nothing; from this knowledge he also procures the horrible pleasure of having to die, of the ordering of his own life. He recognizes that his death consists in having to live before God without life from God, that he is really man *sicut deus* who is condemned to live without life. Fallen into death, man constantly perverts this knowledge into the pleasure of the permission to die. This final reality of the death of Adam can only be expressed in the following paradoxical statement: The will to live, the inability to live, having to live—that is the living death of the man who is like God. This life of Adam's is a continued, renewed rebellion against this existence; it is a dispute with life, a reaching out for the life that would bring *this* life to an end, that would be the new life. In all circumstances Adam wants to *live*. To be sure, he is allowed to live in the preserved world but he is intelligent, he knows that this life is life on the way to death and is therefore death. Now his lust for life is without measure, in the death of being like God a nameless thirst for life grips him. This thirst takes on a strange form. The desperate feature of Adam's situation is just that he lives out of himself, he is imprisoned within himself, and thus he can only desire himself, he can only crave for himself, for he is his own God, he has become the creator of his own life. When he seeks God, when he seeks life, then he only seeks himself. On the other hand it is just his solitude, his reposing in himself, his being in himself that plunges him into an unquenchable thirst. In the nature of the case it is a desperate, unquenchable, eternal thirst that Adam feels for life, that the more passionately Adam asks for life the more deeply he is entangled in death. It is a thirst for death. Therefore Adam's thirst for life is perverse. Languishing without life Adam wants his own death, perhaps so that death may give him life. Then and today Adam does not want eternal life, so far as he understands himself as Adam. He wants death, he wants to die—which one of us wants to live eternally? But just in this death Adam hopes to be able to save his life from the servitude of having to live without life. It is thus flight from life and reaching out for life at the same time, because it is flight from God and search for God in one. It is both the desire to be *sicut deus* and reaching out for the tree of life. But this is now finally barred to him. Adam is *sicut deus*, but as such he is in death. Adam has eaten of the tree of knowledge, but the thirst for the tree of life, which this fruit has given him, remains unquenched. The limit that divides Adam's field from paradise shall from now on be here— where stands the tree of life.

◆ ◆ ◆

He drove out the man; and at the east of the garden of Eden he placed the cherubim, and a flaming sword[1] *which turned every way, to guard the way to the tree of life.*

The limit has not shifted, it is where it always was, in the unenterable middle of the tree of life. But now Adam stands in another place; this limit is no longer in the middle of his life, but it afflicts him from outside, he must continually run against it, it always stands in his way. The German fairy tale of the Sleeping Beauty differs from the story told here by the fact that because of the cutting, flaming sword of the cherubim, no living human being makes his way across. The tree of life is guarded by the power of death, it remains untouchable, divinely unapproachable. But Adam's life before the gate is a continuous attack upon the realm from which he is excluded. It is a flight and a search upon the cursed ground to find what he has lost, and then a repeated, desperate rage against

[1] The German Bible reads "die Cherubim mit dem blossen, hauenden Schwert"="the Cherubim with the naked, cutting sword." [Tr.]

the power with the flaming sword. That this sword of the guard cuts, that it is sharp—this the biblical writer says, not without reason; Adam knows this, he feels it himself time and again: but the gate remains shut.

PART 4

I.

CAIN

4.1 Now Adam knew Eve his wife, and she conceived and bore Cain.

This verse necessarily belongs to what has gone before. Adam and Eve, the human beings *sicut deus,* who have fallen into death, stand the test of their community in a new way. They become the proud creators of new life, but this new life is created in the lustful intercourse of man and death; Cain is the first man to be born upon the cursed ground. The whole story of death begins with Cain. Adam, preserved on the way to death and consumed with thirst for life, begets Cain, the murderer. The new thing about Cain, the son of Adam, is that as man *sicut deus* Cain himself lays violent hands on human life. The man who is not allowed to eat of the tree of life all the more greedily reaches out for the fruit of death, the destruction of life. Only the Creator can destroy life. Cain usurps this ultimate right of the Creator and becomes a murderer. Why does Cain murder? Out of hatred towards God. This hatred is great. Cain is great, he is greater than Adam, for his hatred is greater, and this means that his yearning for life is greater. The story of death stands under the mark of Cain.

Christ on the Cross, the murdered Son of God, is the end of the story of Cain, and thus the actual end of the story. This is the last desperate storming of the gate of paradise. And under the flaming sword under the Cross, mankind dies. But Christ lives. The stem of the Cross becomes the staff of life, and in the midst of the world life is set up anew upon the cursed ground. In the middle of the world the spring of life wells up on the wood of the cross and those who thirst for life are called to this water, and those who have eaten of the wood of this life shall never hunger and thirst again. What a strange paradise is this hill of Golgotha, this Cross, this blood, this broken body! What a strange tree of life, this tree on which God himself must suffer and die—but it is in fact the Kingdom of Life and of the Resurrection given again by God in grace; it is the opened door of imperishable hope, of waiting and of patience. The tree of life, the Cross of Christ, the middle of the fallen and preserved world of God, for us that is the end of the story of paradise.

> *He unlocks again the door*
> *Of paradise today:*
> *The angel guards the gate no more.*
> *To God our thanks we pay.*

Temptation

NOTE

From April 12-17, 1937, there was a reunion of the clergy who two years earlier, under the leadership of Dietrich Bonhoeffer, had established the seminary of the Confessing Church in Finkelwalde, near Stettin, and had finished the first course. Dietrich Bonhoeffer introduced each day with a Bible study on Temptation. The manuscript survived, and needed only to be put in order.

E. B.

I.

LEAD US NOT INTO TEMPTATION

Preliminary

ABANDONMENT

Lead us not into temptation. Natural man and moral man cannot understand this prayer. Natural man wants to prove his strength in adventure, in struggle, in encounter with the enemy. That is life. "If you do not stake your life you will never win it." Only the life which has run the risk of death is life which has been won. That is what natural man knows. Moral man also knows that his knowledge is true and convincing only when it is tried out and proved, he knows that the good can live only from evil, and that it would not be good but for evil. So moral man calls out evil, his daily prayer is—Lead me into temptation, that I may test out the power of the good in me.

If temptation were really what natural man and moral man understand by it, namely, testing of their own strength— whether their vital or their moral or even their Christian strength—in resistance, on the enemy, then it is true that Christ's prayer would be incomprehensible. For that life is won only from death and the good only from the evil is a piece of thoroughly worldly knowledge which is not strange to the Christian. But all this has nothing to do with the temptation of which Christ speaks. It simply does not touch the reality which is meant here. The temptation of which the whole Bible speaks does not have to do with the testing of my strength, for it is of the very essence of temptation in the Bible that all my strength—to my horror, and without my being able to do anything about it—is turned against me; really all my powers, including my good and pious powers (the strength of my faith), fall into the hands of the enemy power and are now led into the field against me. Before there can be any testing of my powers, I have been robbed of them. "My heart trembles, my strength has left me, and the light of my eyes has departed from me" (Ps. 38.10). This is the decisive fact in the temptation of the Christian, that he is *abandoned*, abandoned by all his powers—indeed, attacked by them— abandoned by all men, abandoned by God himself. His heart shakes, and has fallen into complete darkness. He himself is nothing. The enemy is everything. God has "taken his hand away from him" (*Augsburg Confession*, XIX), "He has left him for a little while" (Isa. 54.7). The man is alone in his temptation. Nothing stands by him. For a little while the devil has room. How is the abandoned man to face the devil? How can he protect himself? It is the prince of this world who opposes him. The hour of the fall has come, the irrevocable, eternal fall: for who will free us again from the clutches of Satan?

A defeat shows the physical and the moral man that his powers have to increase before they can withstand the trial. So his defeat is never irrevocable. The Christian knows that in every hour of temptation all his strength will leave him. For him temptation means a dark hour which can be irrevocable. He does not seek for his strength to be proved, but he prays, "Lead us not into temptation." So the biblical meaning of temptation is not a testing of strength, but the loss of all strength, defenceless deliverance into Satan's hands.

THE OCCASION

Temptation is a concrete happening which juts out from the course of life. For the physical man all life is a struggle, and for the moral man every hour is a time of temptation. The Christian knows hours of temptation, which differ from hours of gracious care and preservation from temptation as the devil is different from God. The saying that every moment of life is a time of decision is for him a meaningless abstraction. The Christian cannot see his life as a series of principles, but only in its relation to the living God. The God who causes day and night to be gives also seasons of thirst and seasons of refreshment; he gives storms and peace, times of grief and fear, and times of joy. "Weeping may tarry for the night, but joy cometh in the morning" (Ps. 30.5). "To every thing there is a season, and a time to every purpose under the heaven: a time to be born, and a time to die; a time to plant, and a time to pluck up that which is planted; a time to kill, and a time to heal; a time to break down, and a time to build up; a time to weep, and a time to laugh. . . . He hath made every thing beautiful in its time" (Eccles. 3.1-4, 11). It is not what life may be in itself, but how God now deals with me, which matters for the Christian. God rejects me, and he accepts me again. He destroys my work, and he builds it up again. "I am the Lord, and there is none else. I form the light, and create darkness; I make peace, and create evil" (Isa. 45.7).

So the Christian lives from the times of God, and not from his own idea of life. He does not say that he lives in constant temptation and constant testing, but in the time when he is preserved from temptation he prays that God may not let the time of temptation come over him.

Suddenly temptation comes upon the pious man. "Suddenly do they shoot at him, and fear not" (Ps. 64.4) at a time when he least expected it. "For man also knoweth not his time . . . even so are the sons of men snared in an evil time, when it falleth suddenly upon them" (Eccles. 9.12). "For suddenly shall the wrath of the Lord come forth, and in thy security thou shalt be destroyed, and perish in the day of vengeance" (Eccles. 5.7). So the Christian recognizes the cunning of Satan. Suddenly doubt has been sowed in his heart, suddenly everything is uncertain, what I do is so meaningless, suddenly sins of long ago are alive in me as though they had happened today, and they torture and torment me, suddenly my whole heart is full of deep sorrow for myself, for the world, for God's powerlessness over me, suddenly my vexation with life will lead me to terrible sin, suddenly evil desire is wakened, and suddenly the Cross is upon me and I tremble. This is the hour of temptation, of darkness, of defenceless deliverance into Satan's hands.

A BOND

But is the hour of temptation not bound to come? So is it not illegitimate to pray in this way? Ought we not rather to pray that in the hour of temptation, which is bound to come, strength may be given us to overcome our temptation? Such a thought claims to know more about temptation than Christ himself, and wants to be better than he who knew the hardest temptation. "Is temptation not bound to come?" Then why? Must God deliver up his own to Satan? Must he lead them to the abyss where they fall? Must God yield such power to Satan? Who are we to speak of temptation is being bound to come? Are we in God's counsel? And if—in virtue of a divine bond which is incomprehensible to us—temptation is bound to come, then Christ, the most tempted of all, summons us to pray against the divine bond—not to yield in stoic resignation to temptation, but to flee from that dark bond, in which God lets the devil do his will, and call to the open divine freedom in which God tramples the devil under foot. "Lead us *not* into temptation."

II.

THE TWO TEMPTATION STORIES

After these preliminary questions we must approach the point of the prayer, "Lead us not into temptation." He who taught the disciples to pray in this way was Jesus Christ, who alone must have known what temptation was. And because he knew he wanted his disciples to pray, "Lead us not into temptation." From the point of view of the temptation of Jesus Christ alone can we understand the meaning of temptation for us.

The Bible is not like a book of edification, telling us many stories of men's temptations and their overcoming. To be precise, the Bible tells only two temptation stories, the temptation of the first man and the temptation of Christ, that is, the temptation which led to man's fall and the temptation which led to Satan's fall. All other temptations in human history have to do with these two stories of temptation. Either we are tempted in Adam or we are tempted in Christ. Either the Adam in me is tempted—in which case we fall. Or the Christ in us is tempted—in which case Satan is bound to fall.

Adam

The temptation of the first man presents the enigma of the
tempter in paradise. We are very prone to look behind that
happening over which the mystery of the unrevealed must
lie, namely the origin of the tempter. From that happening
in paradise we learn three things.

First, that the tempter is to be found wherever there is
innocence. Indeed the tempter is only to be found where
there is innocence; for where there is guilt, he has already
gained power.

Second, it is the quite unmediated appearance of the
tempter in the voice of the serpent in paradise, the presence
of Satan in paradise—in no way established or justified (not
even by any philosophy about Lucifer)—which brings out his
character as seducer. It is the same inscrutable, contingent
suddenness of which we spoke before. The voice of the
tempter does not come out of an abyss only recognized as
"Hell." It completely conceals its origin. It is suddenly near
me and speaks to me. In paradise it is the serpent—quite
plainly a creature of God—through whom the tempter
speaks to Eve. Indeed there is no sign of the origin of the
tempter in fire and brimstone. The denial of the origin belongs to the essence of the seducer.

Third, in order, however, to win access to innocence, it is
necessary that the denial of origin should be maintained until
the end. Innocence means clinging to the Word of God with
pure, undivided hearts. Thus the tempter must introduce
himself in the name of God. He bears with him the Word
of God and expounds it: "Has God really said?" Have you
understood God, the Lord, rightly here? Ought not another
construction to be put on his Word? We cannot imagine the
nameless dread which must have beset the first man in the
face of such a possibility. In front of innocence yawns
the abyss of yet unknown guilt; in front of faith the abyss of
unknown doubts; in front of life the abyss of yet unknown
death. This dread belonging to innocence, which the devil
will rob of its only strength, the Word of God, is the sin of

the seduction. It is not a question of engaging in a struggle, of the freedom of decision for good or for evil—it is not concerned with the ethical concept of seduction. Rather is Adam delivered up defenceless to the tempter. He lacks every insight, power, perception, which would have equipped him for the struggle with this adversary. He is left quite alone. The abyss has opened up beneath him. Only one thing remains: in the midst of this abyss he is upheld by the hand of God, by God's Word. Thus, in the hour of temptation, Adam can only shut his eyes and stand and let himself be upborne by the grace of God. But Adam falls. "Has God really said?" In the abyss of this question Adam sinks and with him the whole of mankind. From the time of Adam's expulsion from paradise every man is born with this question, which Satan has put in Adam's heart. That is the first question of all flesh: "Has God really said?" By this question all flesh comes to fall. The seduction of Adam brings all flesh to death and condemnation.

Christ

In the likeness of sinful flesh the Son of God, Jesus Christ our Saviour, came upon the earth. In him was all desire and all fear of the flesh, all damnation of the flesh and alienation from God. He "hath been in all points tempted like as we are, yet without sin" (Heb. 4.15). If he was to help man, who is flesh, he had to take upon himself the whole temptation experience of the flesh. Even Jesus Christ κατὰ σάρκα was born with the question: "Has God really said?"—yet without sin.

The temptation of Christ was harder, unspeakably harder, than the temptation of Adam; for Adam carried nothing in himself which could have given the tempter a claim and power over him. But Christ bore in himself the whole burden of the flesh, under the curse, under condemnation; and yet his temptation was henceforth to bring help and salvation to all flesh.

The Gospel reports that Jesus was led up of the Spirit

into the wilderness to be tempted of the devil (Matt. 4.1). Therefore the temptation does not begin with the Father equipping the Son with every power and every weapon, in order that he might be victorious in the struggle; but the Spirit leads Jesus into the wilderness, into solitude, into abandonment. God takes from his Son all help of man and creature. The hour of temptation must find Jesus weak, lonely, and hungry. God leaves man alone in temptation. So Abraham had to be quite alone on the mountain in Moriah. Yes, God himself abandons man in face of temptation. Only thus can one understand II Chron. 32.31: "God left Hezekiah to try him," or the Psalmists' repeated cry: "God, forsake me not" (Ps. 38.21; 71.9, 18; 119.8). "Hide not thy face from me;. . . . cast me not off, neither forsake me, O God of my salvation" (Ps. 27.9)—which must be incomprehensible to all human-ethical-religious thinking. God shows himself in temptation not as the gracious, the near one, who furnishes us with all the gifts of the Spirit; on the contrary he forsakes us, he is quite distant from us; we are in the wilderness. (Later we shall have more to say about this.)

In distinction from the temptation of Adam and all human temptations the tempter himself comes to Jesus (Matt. 4.3). Whereas elsewhere he makes use of creatures, here he himself must conduct the struggle. This makes it clear that in the temptation of Jesus it is a matter of the whole. It is here that the fullest denial of the origin of the tempter is to be found. It may be with reference to the denial of Satan's origin and the temptation of Jesus that Paul said: "Even Satan fashioneth himself into an angel of light" (II Cor. 11.14). We should probably not think that Jesus did not recognize Satan, but that Satan was so enticing that, in this way, he purposed to bring about the fall of Jesus.

THE TEMPTATION OF THE FLESH

Jesus has fasted forty days in the wilderness, and he is hungry. Then came the seducer to him. The tempter begins with the acknowledgment of Jesus as the Son of God. He does not say: "Thou art the Son of God"—he cannot say that!—But he says: If thou art the Son of God, thou who sufferest hunger, command that these stones become bread. Here Satan tempts Jesus in the weakness of his human flesh. He wishes to set his Godhead against his manhood. He plans to make the flesh rebellious towards the spirit. Satan knows that the flesh is afraid of suffering. But why should the Son of God suffer in the flesh? The purpose of this question is clear, Were Jesus in the power of his Godhead to withdraw from suffering in the flesh, all flesh would be lost. The way of the Son of God on earth would be at an end. The flesh would once more belong to Satan. Jesus' answer with the Word of God shows, first of all, that even the Son of God stands under the Word of God, and that he can and will claim no individual right beside this Word. Secondly, it shows that Jesus will rely on this Word alone. The flesh, too, belongs to the Word of God, and if it must suffer, this means that man does not live by bread alone. Jesus has preserved his manhood and his way of suffering in temptation. The first temptation is the temptation of the flesh.

SPIRITUAL TEMPTATION

In the second temptation Satan begins as in the first: If thou art the Son of God—but he piles on his temptation by himself quoting God's Word against Jesus. Even Satan can use God's Word in the struggle. Jesus has to allow his Sonship to be attested. He is to demand a sign from God. That is the temptation of Jesus' faith, the temptation of the spirit. If the Son of God is to be in the midst of men's suffering, then ask for a sign of the power of God, which can save him at any time. Jesus' answer sets God's Word against God's Word, but in such a way that there is no fatal uncertainty, and so that truth is set against lies. Jesus calls this temptation a temptation of God. He will remain only by his Father's Word; that suffices him. If he had wanted more than this Word, he would have given place in himself to doubt in God. Faith which demands more than the Word of God in precept and promise, becomes a temptation of God. To tempt God means to lay upon God himself guilt, unfaithfulness and falsehood, instead of upon Satan. To tempt God is the highest spiritual temptation.

COMPLETE TEMPTATION

Satan comes differently the third time—without the declaration about the Sonship, without the Word of God. He comes now—and that is the decisive thing—in his wholly unconcealed display of power as the prince of this world. Now Satan fights with his very own weapons. There is no more veiling, no more dissimulation. Satan's power matches itself directly against the power of God. Satan hazards his ultimate resources. His gift is immeasurably big and beautiful and alluring; and in return for this gift he claims—worship. He demands open apostasy from God, whose only justification is the size and beauty of Satan's kingdom. This temptation shows with great clarity and insight completely final denial of God and submission to Satan. It is the temptation to the sin against the Holy Ghost.

Because Satan has fully revealed himself, he must be addressed, encountered and rejected by Jesus: "Get thee hence Satan; for it is written, Thou shalt worship the Lord thy God, and him only shalt thou serve."

Jesus is tempted in his flesh, in his faith and in his allegiance to God. All three are the one temptation—to separate Jesus from the Word of God. The nature of the flesh is used by Satan against the divine command. If Satan once gets power over the flesh of Jesus, Jesus will be in his hands. If Jesus will not rely on the Word alone, only believing, blindly believing and obeying, he is no longer the Christ and redeemer of men who can only find salvation through faith in the Word. So Satan has tempted the flesh and spirit of Jesus against the Word of God. The third temptation attacks the whole physical-spiritual existence of the Son of God. "If thou dost not want to be inwardly torn by me, give me the whole of thyself—and I will make thee great in this world, in hatred of God and in power against him." Thus Jesus suffers the temptation of the flesh, the high spiritual temptation, and, finally, the complete temptation, and in all three only the one temptation of the Word of God.

The temptation of Jesus is not that heroic struggle of man against wicked powers that we fondly and lightly suppose. In the temptation Jesus is robbed of all his own strength, he is left alone by God and man, in anguish he must suffer Satan's robbery, he has fallen into the deepest darkness. He is left with nothing but the saving, supporting, enduring Word of God, which holds him firmly and which fights and conquers for him. The night of the last words of Jesus—"My God, my God, why hast thou forsaken me"—has fallen, it must follow the hour of this temptation as the last fleshly-spiritual, complete temptation of the Saviour. The suffering by Jesus of abandonment by God and man is God's Word and judgment for him. In his defenceless, powerless submission to the power of Satan the reconciliation arises. He was tempted like as we are—yet without sin.

Thus, in the temptation of Jesus, there really remains nothing except God's Word and promise, no native strength and joy for the fight against wickedness, only God's strength and victory, which holds fast in the Word, and the Word robs Satan of his power. Only by God's Word is the temptation overcome.

"Then the devil leaveth him." As in the beginning God had abandoned him, now the tempter abandons him—"and behold angels came and ministered unto him." In the Garden of Gethsemane, too, "there appeared unto him an angel from heaven, strengthening him" (Luke 22.43). That is the end of the temptation, that he who has entered into all weakness but who has been upheld by the Word, receives from an angel of God refreshment of all his powers of body, soul and spirit.

III.

THE TEMPTATION OF CHRIST IN HIS PEOPLE

The Taking Over of the Temptations

By the temptation of Jesus Christ the temptation of Adam is brought to an end. As in Adam's temptation all flesh fell so in the temptation of Jesus Christ all flesh has been snatched away from the power of Satan. For Jesus Christ wore our flesh, he suffered our temptation, and he won the victory from it. Thus today we all wear the flesh which in Jesus Christ vanquished Satan. Both our flesh and we have conquered in the temptation of Jesus. Because Christ was tempted and overcame, we can pray: Lead us not into temptation. For the temptation has already come and been conquered. He did it in our stead. "Look on the temptation of thy Son Jesus Christ and lead *us* not into temptation." Of the granting of that prayer we may and should be certain; we should utter our amen to it, for it *is* granted in Jesus Christ himself. From henceforth *we* shall no longer be led into temptation, but every temptation which happens now is the temptation of Jesus Christ in his members, in his congregation. We are not tempted, *Jesus Christ is tempted in us.*

Because Satan could not bring about the fall of the Son of God, he pursues him now with all temptations in his members. But these last temptations are only the off-shoots of the temptation of Jesus on earth; for the power of temptation is broken in the temptation of Jesus. His disciples are to let themselves be found in this temptation, and then the kingdom is assured to them. It is the fundamental word of Jesus to all his disciples. "But ye are they which have continued with me in my temptations, and I appoint unto you a kingdom" (Luke 22.28f.). It is not the temptations of the *disciples* which here receive the promise, but their participation in the life and the temptation of Jesus. The temptations of the disciples fall on *Jesus*, and the temptations of Jesus come upon the disciples. But to share in the atonement of Christ means to share also in Christ's overcoming and victory. It does not mean that the temptations of Christ had finished and that the disciples would no longer suffer them. They will indeed suffer temptations, but it will be the temptations of Jesus Christ which befall them. Christ has also won the victory over these temptations.

It is by the disciples sharing in the temptation of Jesus Christ that Jesus will protect his disciples from other temptation: "Watch and pray that ye enter not into temptation" (Matt. 26.41). What temptation threatened the disciples in the hour of Gethsemane if it was not that they should be offended at the passion of Christ and they would not share in his temptations? So Jesus uses here the petition of the Lord's Prayer: "Lead us not into temptation." Finally it is the same thing when it says in Hebrews 2.18: "For in that he himself hath suffered being tempted, he is able to succour them that are tempted." This is not only a question of the help which he alone can give who has learnt to know the need and suffering of the other man in his own experience. The true meaning is rather that in my temptations my real succour is only in his temptation; to share in his temptation is the only help in my temptation. Thus I ought not to think of my temptation other than as the temptation of Jesus Christ. In his temptation is my succour; for here only is victory and overcoming.

The practical task of the Christian must, therefore, be to understand all the temptations which come upon him as temptations of Jesus Christ in him, and thus he will be aided. But how does it happen? Before we can speak of the concrete temptations of Christians and their overcoming, the question of the author of the temptation of Christians must be put. Only when the Christian knows with whom he has to do in temptation, can he act rightly in the actual event.

The Three Authors of Temptation

The Holy Scriptures call the different authors of the temptation: the devil, the lust of man, God himself.

THE DEVIL

What does the Bible say when it calls the devil the author of temptation? It says, first, that temptation is entirely against God. It is inconceivable, from the character of God, that men should be tempted by God to doubt in God's Word and to apostasy. The tempter is always the enemy of God. Secondly, the enemy of God shows in temptation his power to do something that is not the will of God. What no creature could do for himself, that the wicked enemy can do, that is to say that the temptation is a *power* which is stronger than any creature. It is the invasion of Satan's power into the world of creation. If the devil is the tempter, no creature can withstand temptation in his own strength. He must fall. So great is the power of Satan (Eph. 6.12). Thirdly, the temptation is seduction, leading astray. Therefore it is of the devil; for the devil is a liar. "When he speaketh a lie, he speaketh of his own: for he is a liar, and the father thereof" (John 8.44). Sin is a deceit (Heb. 3.13). The deceit, the lie of the devil consists of this, that he wishes to make man believe that he can live without God's Word. Thus he dangles before man's phantasy a kingdom of faith, of power and of peace, into which only he can enter who consents to the temptations; and he conceals from men that he, as the devil, is the most unfortunate and unhappy of beings, since he is finally and eternally rejected by God. Fourthly, temptation comes from the devil;

for here the devil becomes the accuser of man. There are two parts to every temptation: man must be alienated from the Word of God, and God must be forced to reject man, because the accuser has exposed his sins. About this second part we can say this. Job's is the prototype of all temptations. Satan's question is: "Doth Job fear God for nought? Hast not thou made an hedge about him, and about his house, and about all that he hath, on every side? Thou hast blessed the work of his hands, and his substance is increased in the land. But put forth thine hand now, and touch all that he hath, and will he not renounce thee to thy face?" (Job 1.9ff.). Here the meaning of all temptation is clear. Everything that a man has is taken from him, and he is in the end made completely powerless. Poverty, sickness, scorn and rejection by the pious plunge him into darkest night. Everything of which Satan as prince of this world can rob man he takes from him. He drives him into the loneliness in which for the tempted nothing remains but God. And even here it must be made known that man does not fear God for nought, that he does not love God for God's sake but for the sake of the good things of this world. At some place Satan will make it clear that Job does not fear God, love and trust him, above all things. Thus every temptation is a revelation of sin, and the accuser stands there more righteous than God; for he has uncovered sin. He compels God to judge.

So the devil shows himself in temptation as the enemy of God, as power, as a liar and as accuser. For men in temptation it means this: that the enemy of God must be recognized in temptation; that the power which is opposed to God must be overcome in temptation; that the lie must be unmasked in temptation.

As to how this can actually be accomplished, more later. We must ask further questions.

LUST

What does the Bible say about the lust of men as the author of their temptation? "Let no man say when he is tempted, I am tempted of God: for God cannot be tempted with evil, and he himself tempteth no man: but each man is tempted, when he is drawn away by his own lust, and enticed. Then the lust, when it hath conceived, beareth sin: and the sin, when it is fullgrown, bringeth forth death" (James 1.31ff.).

First, he who transfers the guilt of the temptation to someone other than himself, thereby justifies his fall. If I am not guilty in my temptation, neither am I guilty when I perish in it. Temptation is guilt in so far as the fall is inexcusable. It is therefore impossible to put the guilt of temptation on to the devil; then all the more is it a blasphemy to make God answerable for it. It may appear pious, but in truth the statement implies that God is himself in some way open to evil. This would attribute division to God, which makes his Word and his will questionable, ambiguous, doubtful. Since evil has no place in God, not even the possibility of evil, temptation to evil must never be laid at God's door. God himself tempts no one. The source of temptation lies in my own self. Secondly, temptation is punishment. The place in which all temptation originates is my evil desires. My own longing for pleasure, and my fear of suffering, entice me to let go the Word of God. The hereditary depraved nature of the flesh is the source of the evil inclinations of body and soul, as are men and things, which now become temptation. Neither the beauty of the world, nor suffering, are in themselves evil and tempting, but our evil desires which win pleasure from all this and which let themselves be suborned and enticed, turn all this into temptation for us. While in the devilish origin of temptation the objectivity of temptation must become clear, here its complete subjectivity is emphasized. Both are equally necessary.

Thirdly, desire in itself does not make me sinful. But "when it hath conceived, it beareth sin, and the sin, when it is fullgrown, bringeth forth death." Desire conceives by the union of my "I" with it—when I abandon the Word of God which upholds me. As long as desire remains untouched by my self, it is an "It." But sin occurs only through the "I." Thus the source of temptation lies in the ἐπιθυμία, the source of sin is in myself, and in my self alone. Therefore I must acknowledge that mine alone is the guilt and that I deserve eternal death when in temptation I succumb to sin. Jesus indeed pronounces a terrible judgement on him who tempts the innocent, who offends one of the little ones; "Woe unto him who tempts another to sin"—that is what the Word of God says about every tempter. But yours alone is the guilt in your sin and your death, if you submit to the temptation of your desire. That is God's Word to the tempted.

GOD HIMSELF

What does the Bible say about God when it makes him the author of temptation? That is the most difficult and final question. God tempts no one, says James. But the Bible also says that "God did prove Abraham (Gen. 22.1), that Israel was tempted by God (II Chron. 32.31). David at the census was "made angry by the wrath of God" (II Sam. 24.1), "by Satan"—according to I Chron. 21.1. Likewise in the New Testament the temptation of Christians is looked upon as the judgement of God (I Pet. 4.12, 17). What does it all mean?

First, the Bible makes it clear that nothing can happen on earth without the will and permission of God. Satan also is in God's hands. He must—against his will—serve God. It is true that Satan has power, but only where God "allows it to him. There is consolation for the tempted believer. Satan had to ask permission from God for Job's temptation. He can do nothing on his own. Thus God must first abandon man in order that Satan may have opportunity for temptation— "God left Hezekiah to try him" (II Chron. 32.31). This is how we should understand everything that was said earlier about the abandonment of the tempted. God gives the tempted into Satan's hands.

Second—the child's question: "Why doesn't God simply strike Satan dead?" demands an answer. We know that the same question can mean: Why must Christ be tempted, suffer and die? Why must Satan have such power over him? God gives Satan opportunity because of men's sin. Satan must execute the death of the sinner; for only if the sinner dies, can the righteous man live; only if the old man daily and wholly perishes, can the new man rise from the dead. While Satan thus employs himself, he serves God's purpose. "The Lord killeth, and maketh alive: He bringeth down to the grave, and bringeth up" (I Sam. 2.6). So must Satan unwillingly serve God's plan of redemption; with Satan rests death and sin, but with God life and righteousness. Satan does his work in three ways in temptation. He leads men to the knowledge of sin. He allows the flesh to suffer. He gives death to the sinner.

1. "God left him, to try him, that he might know all that was in his heart" (II Chron. 32.31). The heart of man is revealed in temptation. Man knows his sin, which without temptation he could never have known; for in temptation man knows on what he has set his heart. The coming to light of sin is the work of the accuser, who thereby thinks to have won the victory. But it is sin which is become manifest which can be known and therefore forgiven. Thus the manifestation of sin belongs to the salvation plan of God with man, and Satan must serve this plan.

2. In temptation Satan wins power over the believer as far as he is flesh. He torments him by enticement to lust, by the pains of privation, and by bodily and spiritual suffering of every kind. He robs him of everything he has and, at the same time, entices him to forbidden happiness. He drives him, like Job, into the abyss, into the darkness, in which the tempted one is only sustained by the grace of God which he does not perceive and feel, but which nevertheless holds him fast. So Satan appears to have won full power over the believer, but this victory turns to complete defeat. For the mortification of the flesh is indeed the way to life in judgement; and the tempted one, in being driven into a complete void and into defencelessness, is driven by Satan directly into the very hands of God. Thus Christ recognizes at once in Satan's fury the gracious chastening of God (Heb. 12.4ff.), of the Father to his child; the gracious judgement of God which preserves man from the judgement of wrath. The hour of temptation, therefore, becomes the hour of greatest joy (James 1.2ff.).

3. The last enemy is death. Death is in Satan's hands. The sinner dies. Death is the last temptation. But even here where man loses everything, where hell reveals its terror, even here life has broken in upon the believer. Satan loses his last power and his last right over the believer. We ask once more: Why does God give Satan opportunity for temptation? First, in order finally to overcome Satan. Through getting his rights Satan is destroyed. As God punishes the godless man by allowing him to be godless, and allowing him his right and his freedom, and as the godless man perishes in this freedom of his (Rom. 1.19ff.), so God does not destroy Satan by an act of violence, but Satan must destroy himself. Second, God gives opportunity to Satan in order to bring believers to salvation. Only by knowledge of sin, by suffering and death, can the new man live. Third, the overcoming of Satan and the salvation of believers is true and real in Jesus Christ alone. Satan plagues Jesus with all sins, all suffering and the death of mankind. But with that his power is at an end. He had taken everything from Jesus Christ and thereby delivered him to God alone. Thus we are led to the knowledge from which we set out: Believers must learn to understand all their temptations as the temptation of Jesus Christ in them. In this way they will share in the victory.

But how can the Bible say that God tempts man? It speaks of the wrath of God, of which Satan is the executor (cf. II Sam. 24.1; I Chron. 21.1). The wrath of God lay upon Jesus Christ from the hour of the temptation. It struck Jesus because of the sin of the flesh which he wore. And because the wrath of God found obedience, for the sake of sin, obedience even unto the righteous death of him who bore the sin of the whole world, the wrath was propitiated, the wrath of God had driven Jesus to the gracious God, the grace of God had overcome the wrath of God, the power of Satan was conquered. But where the whole temptation of the flesh, all the wrath of God is obediently endured in Jesus Christ, there the temptation is conquered in Jesus Christ, there the Christian finds behind the God of wrath who tempts him the God of grace who tempts no one.

IV

CONCRETE TEMPTATIONS AND
THEIR CONQUEST

In the concrete temptation of Christ there is also, therefore, to be distinguished the hand of the devil and the hand of God; there is the question of resistance and of submission in the right place, that is, resistance to the devil is only possible in the fullest submission to the hand of God.

This must now be made clear in detail. Since all temptations of believers are temptations of Christ in his members, of the body of Christ, we speak of these temptations in the analogy of the temptation of Christ. (1) Of fleshly temptation. (2) Of high spiritual temptations. (3) Of the last temptation. But I Cor. 10.12ff. is true of all temptations: "Wherefore let him that thinketh he standeth take heed lest he fall. There hath no temptation taken you but such as man can bear: but God is faithful, who will not suffer you to be tempted above that ye are able; but will with the temptation make also the way of escape, that ye may be able to endure it." Here St. Paul opposes first all false security and, secondly, all false despondency in face of temptation. No one can be sure even for a moment that he can remain free from temptation. There is no temptation which could not attack me suddenly at this moment. No one can think that Satan is far from him. "Be sober, be watchful: your adversary the devil, as a roaring lion, walketh about, seeking whom he may devour." (I Pet. 5.8). Not for one moment in this life are we secure from temptation and fall. Therefore do not be proud if you see another stumble and fall. Such security will be a snare for you. "Be not high-minded, but fear" (Rom. 11.20). Rather be at all time ready that the tempter find no power in you.

"Watch and pray, that ye enter not into temptation" (Matt. 26.41). Be on your guard against the crafty enemy, pray to God that he hold us fast in his Word and his grace—that is the attitude of the Christian towards temptation.

But the Christian must not be afraid of temptation. If it comes upon him in spite of watching and praying, then he should know that he can conquer every temptation. There is no temptation which cannot be conquered. God knows our abilities, and he will not let us be tempted beyond our power. It is *human* temptation which harasses us, that is to say, it is not too big for us men. God allots to every man that portion which he can bear. That is certain. He who loses courage because of the suddenness and the awfulness of temptation, has forgotten the main point, namely that he will quite certainly withstand the temptation because God will not let it go beyond that which he is able to endure. There are temptations by which we are particularly frightened because we are so often wrecked upon them. When they are suddenly there again, we so often give ourselves up for lost from the beginning. But we must look at these temptations in the greatest peace and composure, for they can be conquered and they are conquered, so certain is it that God is faithful. Temptation must find us in humility and in certainty of victory.

The Temptations of the Flesh

We speak first of temptation by desire and then of temptation by suffering.

DESIRE

In our members there is a slumbering inclination towards desire which is both sudden and fierce. With irresistible power desire seizes mastery over the flesh. All at once a secret, smouldering fire is kindled. The flesh burns and is in flames. It makes no difference whether it is sexual desire, or ambition, or vanity, or desire for revenge, or love of fame and power, or greed for money, or, finally, that strange desire for the beauty of the world, of nature. Joy in God is in course of being extinguished in us and we seek all our joy in the creature. At this moment God is quite unreal to us, he loses all reality, and only desire for the creature is real; the only reality is the devil. Satan does not here fill us with hatred of God, but with forgetfulness of God. And now his falsehood is added to this proof of strength. The lust thus aroused envelops the mind and will of man in deepest darkness. The powers of clear discrimination and of decision are taken from us. The questions present themselves: "Is what the flesh desires really sin in this case?" "Is it really not permitted to me, yes—expected of me, now, here, in my particular situation, to appease desire?" The tempter puts me in a privileged position as he tried to put the hungry Son of God in a privileged position. I boast of my privilege against God.

It is here that everything within me rises up against the Word of God. Powers of the body, the mind and the will, which were held in obedience under the discipline of the Word, of which I believed that I was the master, make it clear to me that I am by no means master of them. "All my powers forsake me," laments the psalmist. They have all gone over to the adversary. The adversary deploys my powers against me. In this situation I can no longer act as a hero; I am a defenceless, powerless man. God himself has forsaken me. Who can conquer, who can gain the victory?

None other than the Crucified, Jesus Christ himself, for whose sake all this happens to me; for he is by me and in me, and therefore temptation besets me as it beset him.

There is only one stronger reality to be set against the

exclusive reality of desire and of Satan: the image and the presence of the Crucified. Against this power the power of desire breaks up into nothingness; for here it is conquered. Here the flesh has received its right and its reward, namely death. Here I realize that the lust of the flesh is nothing else than the anguish of the flesh in the face of death. Because Christ is the death of the flesh, and because this Christ is within me, the dying flesh rears itself up against Christ. Now I know that the death of the flesh is manifested in the temptation of the flesh. The flesh dies because it kindles lust and desire. In the temptation of the flesh I share in the death of Jesus in the flesh. So the temptation of the flesh which draws me into the death of the flesh, drives me into the death of Christ, who died in the flesh but who is raised in the spirit. Only the death of Christ rescues me from the temptation of the flesh.

Therefore the Bible teaches us in times of temptation in the flesh to *flee:* "Flee fornication" (I Cor. 6.18)—"from idolatry" (I Cor. 10.14)—"youthful lusts" (II Tim. 2.22)—"the lust of the world" (II Pet. 1.4). There is no resistance to Satan other than flight. Every struggle against lust in one's own strength is doomed to failure. Flee—that can indeed only mean, Flee to that place where you find protection and help, flee to the Crucified. His image and his presence alone can help. Here we see the crucified body and perceive in it the end of all desire; here we see right through Satan's deceit and here our spirit again becomes sober and aware of the enemy. Here I perceive the forsakenness and abandonment of my fleshly condition and the righteous judgement of God's wrath on all flesh. Here I know that in this lost condition I could never have helped myself against Satan, but that it is the victory of Jesus Christ which I now share. But here also I find ground for the attitude in which alone I can conquer all temptations—for patience (James 1.2ff.). I ought not to rebel against the temptations of the flesh in unlawful pride, as though I were too good for them. I ought to and I can humble myself under the hand of God and endure patiently the humiliation of such temptations. So I discern in the midst

of Satan's deadly work the righteous and merciful punishment of God. In the death of Jesus I find refuge from Satan
and the communion of death in the flesh under temptation
and of life in the spirit through his victory.

SUFFERING

This makes it clear that temptation by desire means to the
Christian not desire but suffering. Temptation to desire always includes the renunciation of the desire, that is to say,
suffering. Temptation to suffering always includes the longing
for freedom from suffering, that is to say, for desire. Thus
temptation of the flesh through desire and through suffering
is at bottom one and the same.

We shall speak first of the temptation of the Christian
through general sufferings, that is through sickness, poverty,
need of all kinds; after that, of the temptation of the Christian
through suffering for the sake of Christint.

♦ ♦ ♦

GENERAL SUFFERING. If the Christian should fall into
serious sickness, bitter poverty or other severe suffering, he
should know that the devil has his hand in the game. Stoical
resignation, which accepts everything as inevitable, is a self-
defence of the man who will not acknowledge the devil and
God. It has nothing to do with faith in God. The Christian
knows that suffering in this world is linked with the fall of
man, and that God does not will sickness, suffering and
death. The Christian perceives in suffering a temptation of
Satan to separate him from God. It is here that murmuring
against God has its origin. While God disappears from man's
sight in the fire of lust, the heat of affliction easily leads him
into conflict with God. The Christian threatens to doubt the
love of God. Why does God allow this suffering? God's justice
is incomprehensible to him. Why must it happen to me?
What have I done to deserve it? By suffering God should
become our joy. Job is the Biblical prototype of this temptation. Everything is taken from Job by Satan, in order that in
the end he may curse God. Violent pain, hunger and thirst

can rob man of all his strength and lead him to the edge of apostasy.

How does the Christian conquer the temptation of suffering? Here the end of the Book of Job is a great help to us. In the face of suffering Job has protested his innocence to the last, and has brushed aside the counsels to repentance from his friends who try to trace his misfortune back to a particular, perhaps hidden sin of Job. In addition, Job has spoken high-sounding words about his own righteousness. After the appearance of God Job declares: "Therefore have I uttered that which I understood not. . . . wherefore I abhor myself, and repent in dust and ashes" (Job 42.3, 6). But the wrath of God is not now turned against Job, but against his friends: "for ye have not spoken of me the thing that is right, as my servant Job hath" (Job 42.7). Job gets justice before God and yet confesses his guilt before God. That is the solution of the problem. Job's suffering has its foundation not in his guilt but in his righteousness. Job is tempted because of his piety. So Job is right to protest against suffering coming upon him as if he were guilty. Yet this right comes to an end for Job when he no longer faces man but faces God. Face to face with God, even the good, innocent Job knows himself to be guilty.

This means for the Christian, tempted by suffering, that he must and should protest against suffering in so far as, in doing so, he protests against the devil and asserts his own innocence. The devil has broken into God's order and is the cause of suffering (Luther on Lenchen's death!). But in the presence of God the Christian also sees his sufferings as judgement on the sin of all flesh, which also dwells in his own flesh. He recognizes his sin and confesses himself to be guilty. "Thine own wickedness shall correct thee, and thy backslidings shall reprove thee. Know therefore and see that it is an evil thing and a bitter, that thou hast forsaken the Lord thy God, and that my fear is not in thee, saith the Lord, the Lord of hosts" (Jer. 2.19; 4.18). Suffering, therefore, leads to the knowledge of sin, and thereby, to the return to God. We see our suffering as the judgement of God on our flesh, and because of that we can be grateful for it. For judgement on the flesh, the death of the old man is only the side turned towards the world of the life of the new man. Thus it is said: "He that hath suffered in the flesh hath ceased from sin" (I Pet. 4.1). All suffering must lead the Christian to the strengthening of his faith and not to defection. While the flesh shuns suffering and rejects it, the Christian sees his suffering as the suffering of Christ in him. For he has borne our griefs and carried our sorrows. He bore God's wrath on sin. He died in the flesh, and so we also die in the flesh, because he lives in us.

Now the Christian understands his suffering, also, as the temptation of Christ in him. That leads him into patience, into the silent, waiting endurance of temptation, and fills him with gratitude; for the more the old man dies, the more certainly lives the new man; the deeper man is driven into suffering, the nearer he comes to Christ. Just because Satan took everything from Job, he cast him on God alone. So for the Christian suffering becomes a protest against the devil, a recognition of his own sin, the righteous judgement of God, the death of his old man, and communion with Jesus Christ.

♦♦♦

SUFFERING FOR CHRIST'S SAKE. Whereas the Christian must endure the sufferings of this world, just like the godless, there is reserved for the Christian a suffering of which the world knows nothing: suffering for the sake of the Lord Jesus Christ (I Pet. 4.12, 17). This suffering, too, happens to him as temptation (πρὸς πειρασμόν, I Pet. 4.12; cf. Judg. 2.22). While the Christian can understand all general sufferings as consequences of the general sin of the flesh, in which he too shares, the fact of his suffering on account of his righteousness, on account of his faith, must indeed seem strange to him. That the righteous man suffers on account of his sin is understandable; but that the righteous man suffers for the sake of righteousness, that can easily lead him to the stumbling-block in Jesus Christ. Temptation here is so much the greater than in the suffering which is common to all (sickness, poverty, etc.), which cannot be avoided, because this suffering for Christ's sake would end immediately with the denial of Christ. It is therefore to some extent voluntary suffering from which I can escape again. And just here Satan has a free field of operation. He stirs up the longing of the flesh for happiness, he makes the good insights of the Christian take up arms against him, so that he can show the Christian the folly and the wickedness of his voluntary suffering, the pious way out, the special solution of his conflict. Unavoidable suffering is indeed a severe temptation; but much heavier is the suffering which, in the opinion of the world and of my flesh and even of my pious thoughts, is avoidable. The freedom of man is deployed against the bondage of the Christian.

That is a real temptation to apostasy. But the Christian will not be surprised by this temptation; he ought rather to understand that he is here led right into the communion of the sufferings of Christ (I Pet. 4.13). The temptation of the devil drives the Christian afresh into the arms of Jesus Christ, the Crucified. At the very point where Satan robs man of his freedom and sets him against Christ, there is the bondage of the Christian in Jesus Christ most gloriously visible. What do we mean when we speak of sharing in the sufferings of Christ? It means first joy (χαίρετε, I Pet. 4.13). It means awareness of innocence where the Christian suffers "as a Christian" (ὡς χριστιανός, I Pet. 4.16). It means a glorifying of God in the name of Christian, which I bear (δοξαζέτω, I Pet. 4.16). The Christian suffers "in the behalf of Christ" (Phil. 1.29). But, finally and essentially, it means the understanding of the judgement which begins at the house of God (I Pet. 4.17). This is a hard thought—that the suffering which I suffer as a Christian, as a righteous man, can also be understood as a judgement upon sin; and simply everything lies in the combination of these two bits of knowledge. A suffering for Christ's sake which acknowledges no element of judgement in it is fanaticism. What kind of a judgement are we thinking of? The *one* judgement of God which came upon Christ and will come upon all flesh in the end—the judgement of God on sin. No man can give himself to Christ without sharing in this judgement of God. For it is that which distinguishes Christ from the world, that he bore the judgement which the world despised and rejected. The difference is not that judgement came not upon Christ but upon the world; it is rather that Christ, the sinless one, bore God's judgement on sin. So to "belong to Christ" means to bow oneself beneath the judgement of God. It is that which distinguishes suffering in the fellowship of Jesus Christ from suffering in the fellowship of any other ethical or political hero. In suffering the Christian recognizes guilt and judgement. What guilt is it over which he recognizes judgement? It is the guilt of all flesh, which the Christian, too, bears until his life's end; but, beyond that, it is at the same time the guilt of the world in Jesus, which falls upon him and which allows him to suffer. Thus his righteous suffering in the fellowship of Jesus Christ becomes vicarious suffering for the world.

But since Christ himself submitted to the judgement of God, he is taken out of the judgement (Isa 53.8), and because Christians now bow themselves beneath the judgement, they are saved from the wrath and judgement to come. "And if the righteous is scarcely saved" (that is, from the temptation which comes upon him in this suffering), "where shall the ungodly and sinner appear?" (I Pet. 4.18). As judgement at the house of God is a judgement of grace on Christians, so the final judgement of wrath must fall upon the godless.

So the Christian recognizes in his suffering for the sake of Jesus Christ, first, the devil and his temptation to fall from Christ; second, the joy, to be allowed to suffer for Christ; third, the judgement of God at the house of God. He knows that he suffers "according to the will of God" (I Pet. 4.19) and, in the fellowship of the cross, he grasps the grace of God.

The Temptations of the Spirit

Jesus repelled the second temptation of Satan with the words "Thou shalt not tempt the Lord thy God." Satan had tempted Jesus to ask for a visible acknowledgement of his divine Sonship, not to let himself be satisfied with God's Word and promise, and to want more than faith. Jesus called such a demand tempting God, that is, the putting to the proof of the faithfulness of God, the truth of God, the love of God, and attributing to God faithlessness, falsehood and lack of love, instead of looking for them in oneself. All temptation which aims directly at our faith in salvation brings us into the danger of tempting God.

The temptations of the spirit, therefore, with which the devil tempts Christians, have a double aim. The believer is to fall into the sin of spiritual pride *(securitas)* or perish in the sin of despair *(desperatio)*. But in both sins there is the one sin of tempting God.

SECURITAS

The devil tempts us in the sin of spiritual pride, in that he deceives us about the seriousness of God's law and of God's wrath. He takes the word of God's grace in his hand and whispers to us, "God is a God of grace, he will not take our sins so seriously." So he awakens in us the longing to sin against God's grace and to assign forgiveness to ourselves even before our sin. He makes us secure in grace. We are God's children, we have Christ and his cross, we are the true church, no evil can now befall us. God will no longer hold us responsible for our sin. What spells ruin for others has no longer any danger for us. Through grace we have a privileged position before God. Here wanton sin threatens grace (Jude 4). Here it says: "Where is the God of judgement?" (Mal. 2.17), and "we call the proud happy; yea, they that work wickedness are built up; yea, they tempt God, and are delivered" (Mal. 3.15). From such talk follows all indolence of the spirit in prayer and in obedience, indifference to the Word of God, the deadening of conscience, the contempt of the good conscience, "shipwreck concerning the faith" (I Tim. 1.19). (Man persists in unforgiven sin and daily piles up guilt upon guilt.) Lastly there follows the complete hardening and obduracy of the heart in sin, in fearlessness and security before God, hypocritical piety (Acts 5.3 and 9). There is no longer any room for repentance, man can no longer obey. This way ends in idolatry. The God of grace has now become an idol which I serve. This is clearly the tempting of God which provokes the wrath of God.

Spiritual pride arises from disregard of the law and of the wrath of God; whether I say that I am able to stand in my own goodness according to the law of God (justification by works); or whether I, through grace, bestow upon myself a privilege to sin (Nomism and Antinomianism). God is tempted in both, because I put to the test the seriousness of his wrath and demand a sign beyond his Word.

DESPERATIO

The temptation to *desperatio,* to despair *(acedia)* corresponds to the temptation to *securitas.* Here not the law and the wrath, but the grace and promise of God are attacked and put to the test. In this way Satan robs the believer of all joy in the Word of God, all experience of the good God; in place of which he fills the heart with the terrors of the past, of the present and of the future. Old long-forgotten guilt suddenly rears up its head before me, as if it had happened today. Opposition to the Word of God and unwillingness to obey assume huge proportions, and complete despair of my future before God overwhelms my heart. God was never with me, God is not with me, God will never forgive me; for my sin is so great that it cannot be forgiven. Thus man's spirit is in rebellion against the Word of God. Man now demands an experience, proof of the grace of God. Otherwise, in his despair of God he will no longer listen to his Word. And this despair drives him either into the sin of blasphemy or into self-destruction, to the extremity of despair, to suicide, like Saul and Judas; or man, in despair of God's grace, will try to create for himself the sign that God refuses him; in his own strength he will be a saint—in defiance of God—in self-annihilating asceticism and works—or even by magic.

In ingratitude, in disobedience, and in hopelessness, man hardens himself against the grace of God. Satan demands a sign that he is a saint. The promise of God in Christ is no longer sufficient. "And that is the hardest and highest temptation and suffering, that God sometimes attacks and exercises his greatest saints—which man is in the habit of calling *desertio gratiae,* when the heart of man feels nothing less than that God has abandoned him with his grace, and he no longer wishes to live." "But it is difficult for the human heart to accept consolation, for when our Lord God heartens a man, his soul wishes to depart from him, his eyes swim with tears and the sweat of fear breaks out." (Luther on Gen. 35.1)

When Satan deploys God's Word in the law against God's Word in Christ, when he becomes the accuser who allows man to find no comfort, then we ought to think of the following: First, it is the devil himself who here puts God's Word into the mouth. Second, we should never argue with the devil about our sins, but we should speak about our sins only with Jesus. Third, we should tell the devil that Jesus has called to himself not the righteous but sinners, and that we—in defiance of the devil—wish to remain sinners in order to be with Jesus rather than be righteous with the devil. Fourth, we should understand how, in such temptation, our own sin is punished by the wrath of God and comes to light; that is, first, our ingratitude in face of everything that God has done for us up to this moment. "Forget not what good he has done you." "Whoso offereth the sacrifice of thanksgiving glorifieth me, and to him . . . will I shew the salvation of God" (Ps. 50.23); second, our present disobedience which will do no penance for unforgiven sin and will not relinquish its favourite sin (For unforgiven, cherished sin is the best gateway by which the devil can invade our hearts); and, finally, our hopelessness, as though our sins were too great for God, as though Christ had suffered only for trivial sins and not for the real and great sins of the whole world, as though God did not still purpose great things even with me, as though he had not prepared an inheritance in heaven even for me. Fifth, I ought to thank God for his judgement on me, which shows me that he "heartens" and loves me. Sixth, I must recognize in all this that I am here thrust by Satan into the highest temptation of Christ on the cross, as he cried: "My God, my God, why hast thou forsaken me." But where God's wrath broke out, there was reconciliation. Where I, smitten by God's wrath, lose everything, there I hear the words: "My grace is sufficient for thee; for my power is made perfect in weakness" (II Cor. 12.9). Lastly, in gratitude for temptation overcome I know, at the same time, that no temptation is more terrible than to be without temptation.

The Last Temptation

As to how Satan repeats the third temptation of Jesus on believers there is not much to be said. Here it is a matter of the unconcealed appearance of Satan, in which he tempts us to a wilful and final defection from God, by promising us, through the worship of Satan, all power and all happiness on this earth. Just as temptations of the spirit are not experienced by all Christians, since they would go beyond their powers, so this last temptation certainly comes only to a very few men. Christ has suffered it and conquered; and who would dare to say that Antichrist and the ἀντίχριστοι must have suffered this temptation and have fallen. Where there is a wilful alliance with Satan through spirit or through blood, there the power has broken in which the Bible describes as wanton sin, for which there is no forgiveness, which tramples underfoot the Son of God, which crucifies the Son of God afresh, the abuse of the Spirit of grace (Heb. 10.26 and 6.6), the sin unto death, for which a man ought no longer to pray (I John 5.16ff.), the sin against the Holy Ghost, for which there is no forgiveness (Matt. 12.31ff.). He who has experienced this temptation and has conquered, has indeed won the victory over all temptations.

V.

THE LEGITIMATE STRUGGLE

All temptation is temptation of Jesus Christ and all victory is victory of Jesus Christ. All temptation leads the believer into the deepest solitude, into abandonment by men and by God. But in this solitude he finds Jesus Christ, man and God. The blood of Christ and the example of Christ and the prayer of Christ are his help and his strength. The Book of Revelation says of the redeemed: "They overcome . . . because of the blood of the lamb" (Rev. 12.11). Not by the spirit, but by the blood of Christ is the devil overcome. Therefore in all temptation we must get back to this blood, in which is all our help. Then, too, there is the image of Jesus Christ which we should look upon in the hour of temptation. "See the end of the Lord" (James 5.11). His patience in suffering is the death of the flesh, the suffering of our flesh is made to seem of small account, we are preserved from all pride and comforted in all sorrow. The prayer of Jesus Christ which he promised to Peter: "Simon, behold, Satan asked to have you, that he might sift you as wheat, but I made supplication for thee" (Luke 22.31) represents our weak prayer before the Father in heaven, who does not allow us to be tempted beyond our powers.

Believers suffer the hour of temptation without defence. Jesus Christ is their shield. And only when it is quite clearly understood that temptation must befall the Godforsaken, then the word can at last be uttered which the Bible speaks about the Christian's struggle. From heaven the Lord gives to the defenceless the heavenly armour before which, though men's eyes do not see it, Satan flees. *He* clothes us with the armour of God, *he* gives into our hand the shield of faith, *he* sets upon our brow the helmet of salvation, *he* gives us the sword of the spirit in the right hand. It is the garment of Christ, the robe of his victory, that he puts upon his struggling community.

The Spirit teaches us that the time of temptations is not yet ended, but that the hardest temptation is still to come to his people. But he promises also: "Because thou didst keep the word of my patience, I also will keep thee from the hour of trial, that hour which is to come upon the whole world, to try them that dwell upon the earth. I come quickly" (Rev. 3.10ff.), and "The Lord knoweth how to deliver the godly out of temptation" (II Pet. 2.9).

So we pray, as Jesus Christ has taught us, to the Father in heaven: "Lead us not into temptation," and we know that our prayer is heard, for all temptation is conquered in Jesus Christ for all time, unto the end. So together with James we say: "Blessed is the man that endureth temptation, for when he hath been approved, he shall receive the crown of life, which the Lord promised to them that love him" (James 1.12). The promise of Jesus Christ proclaims: "Ye are they which have continued with me in my temptations, and I appoint unto you a kingdom" (Luke 22.28f.).